PIRATES
OF
MARYLAND

PIRATES
OF
MARYLAND

PLUNDER AND HIGH ADVENTURE IN THE CHESAPEAKE BAY

Mark P. Donnelly and Daniel Diehl

STACKPOLE BOOKS

Published by
STACKPOLE BOOKS
5067 Ritter Road
Mechanicsburg, PA 17055
www.stackpolebooks.com

Printed in the United States of America

10 9 8 7 6 5 4 3 2 1

FIRST EDITION

Cover design by Wendy Reynolds
Cover photo by Mark P. Donnelly

Library of Congress Cataloging-in-Publication Data

Donnelly, Mark, 1967–
  Pirates of Maryland : plunder and high adventure in the Chesapeake Bay / Mark P. Donnelly and Daniel Diehl. — 1st ed.
    p. cm.
  Includes bibliographical references.
  ISBN 978-0-8117-1041-1 (pbk.)
  1. Pirates—Maryland—Atlantic Coast—Biography. 2. Pirates—Chesapeake Bay (Md. and Va.)—Biography. 3. Pirates—Chesapeake Bay (Md. and Va.)—History. 4. Maryland—History—Colonial period, ca. 1600–1775. 5. Chesapeake Bay (Md. and Va.)—History, Naval. 6. Atlantic Coast (Md.)—History, Naval. I. Diehl, Daniel. II. Title.
  F184.D66 2012
  975.2'02—dc23

2012021115

Contents

Introduction

The history of piracy in North America is rich and diverse, but of the harbors on the Atlantic seaboard, the coastline of Maryland and the Chesapeake Bay saw more nefarious action than most. Why in Maryland? The main ports of trade in North America throughout the first half of the eighteenth century were New York, Boston, Norfolk, Baltimore, and Philadelphia. Many pirates spent their winters raiding the Caribbean and the Spanish Main, then turned north when the weather turned warmer to prey on ships sailing in to American ports from Europe. And it was in these American ports that the pirates were able to sell their stolen Spanish and Caribbean plunder.

We cannot hope to cover the entire history of piracy in Maryland and Chesapeake waters thoroughly in this slim volume, so we have selected representative stories that illustrate this diverse and often overlooked aspect of American history. But before we turn to the subject of piracy in Maryland, let's take a quick look at the general history of piracy in the Western Hemisphere.

No single nation, race, or nationality ever held a monopoly on piracy. Piracy has existed wherever the rewards of the crime have been worth the risk of punishment. It is not difficult to imagine that the earliest humans to put to sea in boats were soon followed by the first pirates. But it was the Europeans of the Atlantic seaboard—the French, Dutch, Spanish, Portuguese, and especially the British—who developed piracy into its most refined form in the late seventeenth and mid-eighteenth centuries.

From time to time, pirates found it profitable to offer their services to nations at war, and in this role they functioned more or less as legal naval auxiliaries under the general name of "privateers." These privateers operated under officially issued "letters of marque," which allowed them to attack any and all enemy shipping. The practice of privateering dates back to the thirteenth century, and it grew in frequency and popularity until it reached its zenith in the late seventeenth century. At this time, Britain and France were almost constantly at war with Spain. Privateers were commissioned to help break Spain's stranglehold on vast swaths of territory and lucrative maritime trade in the Americas. The distinction between these sea wolves and the pirates was, often as not, nothing more than a matter of legal terminology.

From the Caribbean, these sea rovers spread through virtually every sea and ocean around the world like a virus. And they prospered. But pirate plunder was valuable only if it could find a ready market. And it was in North America that the most significant market could be found. During the golden age of piracy (roughly 1680–1730), pirates operated with the active support and cooperation of colonial governors, local officials, merchants, and the general populace of most of the North American colonies. In England, pirates were hunted down relentlessly. In American ports, however, they received protection, hospitality, ships, provisions, crews, counterfeit letters of marque, and most important, a place to sell their ill-gotten booty. Furthermore, by tacitly condoning piracy, the Americans struck a significant blow against British rule in a growing struggle that eventually culminated in the Revolutionary War. By engaging in commerce with pirates, the American colonies could acquire and trade foreign commodities and luxury goods without paying British taxes on their import or delivery.

The illicit complicity between the American colonies and the pirates was widespread by the 1690s. With few exceptions, colonial governors from New England to the Carolinas colluded with the pirates. Boston, New York, and Philadelphia became pirate depots. In fact, the Pennsylvania surveyor of customs reported that the pirates were so brazen in their activities as to have believed themselves almost beyond reproach:

> They walk the streets with their pockets full of gold and are the constant companion of the [heads of] the Government. They threaten my life and those who were active in apprehending them; carry their profitable goods publicly in boats from one place to another for a market; threaten the lives of the King's [tax] collectors and with force and arms rescue the goods from them. All these parts swarm with pirates, so that if some speedy and effectual course be not taken the trade of America will be ruined.

Piracy, for whatever reason a man might adopt it as a lifestyle, was hardly an upwardly mobile career choice. With the many risks a pirate faced, such as dying in battle, contracting one of the rampant diseases that accompanied long periods at sea, or ending up dangling on the end of a rope, the life expectancy of a man once he became a pirate was on average three to five years. So why would any person in his right mind choose such a way of life? The answers were probably as varied as the pirates themselves, but a distillation of the facts provides two explanations that may have accounted for the majority. First, some people simply seem destined for a life of crime and violence. Though the chances of adopting a criminal lifestyle are certainly greater for people from rough backgrounds, sometimes those who grew up with all the advantages still turn to crime. Second, injustices were rampant in seventeenth- and eighteenth-century society. Conditions in the western world's navies were extremely harsh, and some men who had been pressed into service may have turned to piracy after serving under captains who doled out floggings too liberally. Even small infractions of the law could lead to lengthy stays in dungeon-like prisons with virtually no hope of social redemption. For the poor, who were most likely to suffer the injustices of this system, an escape to the sea and piracy might have been the only way out of a dead-end life. The rules that governed most pirate ships were far fairer than those that governed society at large in that era.

Whatever the reasons that drove a man to turn to piracy, he soon found himself among a loose-knit band of desperate men whose lives were short, brutish, and cruel. The stories in this book make no attempt to romanticize the life of a pirate. Some of the men began life as villains and died the same way. Others started out with good intentions and simply went astray. Still others considered themselves patriots and enjoyed the good wishes and support of their countries and neighbors—at least those neighbors who agreed with their cause.

The individuals you will meet in the following pages practiced their illegal trade over the course of more than a century, but all shared certain traits. All of these characters were real, historical people whose lives and deeds are recounted here according to the best historical records available, and all of their exploits and adventures were intertwined with the long, intricate, and rich history of the coastline of Maryland and the Chesapeake Bay.

We hope you enjoy this book and wish you smooth sailing and safe harbors.

William Claiborne

When the British established their first North American colony at Jamestown, Virginia, in 1607, the Spanish Empire took it as a sign of trouble. For decades, the Spanish had held complete control over trade with the Western Hemisphere. The Spanish ambassador in England, Pedro de Zuniga, sent a frantic message to his king, Philip III, stating, "I believe that they [England] would again send people out, because, no doubt, the reason they want that place is its apparent suitability for piracy." His fears were well founded. Multiple locations along the American coastline could be used to launch pirate raids on Spanish shipping vessels, which had been crossing the Atlantic virtually unchallenged for more than a century. Suggestions were even made in the British Parliament that the hundreds of Irish pirates who had been plaguing English shipping could be deported to Virginia to settle, establish colonies, and ply their trade against Spanish vessels.

In 1621, Sir Francis Wyatt arrived in the Chesapeake Bay region to assume command as governor of Virginia. Over the preceding decade, the colony had evolved from a few struggling outposts to a reasonably well-ordered and prosperous state. In all, more than thirteen hundred settlers were busily clearing land for farmsteads and building businesses and new homes. They had finally established peaceful relations with the local native tribes, starvation no longer threatened, the menace of possible Spanish intervention had subsided, and a crop of tobacco was being grown for export.

One of those who had sailed for Virginia on the same ship as Governor Wyatt was a thirty-four-year-old stockholder in the Virginia Company, a well-educated, hearty, and affable but pugnacious man named William Claiborne. Claiborne had been a friend of Jamestown's famous Captain John Smith back in London, and through political connections had secured a three-year appointment as the colony's land surveyor. Claiborne was a man of courage, industry, and resolve, but he could hardly have foreseen the turmoil his personal enterprises would inflict on the political geography and future of the Tidewater region.

William Claiborne became friends with the new governor during the transatlantic crossing and rose rapidly through the ranks of the Virginia colony's governing council. By 1624, he was a valued member of the governor's council, and in 1626, he became secretary of state for Virginia. Claiborne acquired massive tracts of land, but he sought to expand his holdings, as well as those of Virginia, by exploring the head of the Chesapeake River and unknown parts of Virginia and establishing further trade relations with the Indians.

The seaborne leg of Claiborne's expedition began on April 27, 1627, when he sailed northward along the rich, unsettled shorelines of the Chesapeake. It was here that Claiborne first sighted the fertile fields and forests of a large island. He named it Kent Island after his native county of Kent, England, and envisioned it as the perfect base from which to establish a fur-trading empire. The island was nearly three-quarters of the way up the bay; close enough to the mouth of the Susquehanna River to have access to the northern tribes, yet within several days of Jamestown by water. By 1628, Claiborne was actively trading with the Indians and laying the foundations of a successful enterprise.

Less than three years later, with his commission as surveyor complete, Claiborne returned to England to secure financial support for a major trading operation on the Chesapeake. Apparently it did not take much to persuade a wealthy and influential London merchant named William Cloberry to invest heavily in Claiborne's fur-trading enterprise. Cloberry funded a trading company, with Claiborne as a partner and independent manager. While in London,

Claiborne learned of a new colonizing effort being spearheaded by George Calvert, Lord Baltimore, who sought to stake out a portion of the New World as a Catholic stronghold. This would have been of little interest to Claiborne except that Lord Baltimore had his eyes set on a large expanse of coastal land immediately to the north of Virginia—too close for comfort to Claiborne's burgeoning trading empire.

Using Cloberry's influential connections, Claiborne acquired a royal license "to trade and traffic of corne, furs, or any other commodities . . . make discoveries for increase of trade" and "freely conduct said trade with his ships, men, boats and merchandise . . . in all parts of America for which there is not already a patent granted to others for trade." With his license in hand, Claiborne set sail aboard a ship named *Africa* with a cargo of trade goods valued at more than 1,300 pounds sterling and about twenty indentured servants. They landed at Kecoughtan, Virginia, two months later.

At the time of his return, the island at the center of his plans was "unplanted by any man, but possessed of the natives of that country." Claiborne purchased the island from the Indians and proceeded to develop the land, putting a hundred men to work building homes and mills, laying out gardens, planting orchards, and stocking farms with cattle. Within a year, the island had its own representative in the Virginia Assembly.

While Claiborne established a base for his new trading empire, Lord Baltimore continued pressing the British king, Charles I, for a charter to establish his own colony north of Virginia. The colony was to be named Maryland in honor of Queen Henrietta Marie. Lord Baltimore died in April 1632, but his efforts were not in vain. The king agreed to the charter in June, and it was granted to Calvert's eldest son, Cecilius, Second Lord Baltimore.

Unfortunately, the territorial borders assigned to the proposed Maryland colony significantly overlapped areas that had been granted to Virginia colony. To make matters worse, Claiborne's Kent Island lay in the middle of the territory claimed by both Virginia and Maryland. Aware of Claiborne's trading settlement, the new Lord Baltimore initially took a conciliatory approach to the problem. He gave instructions that his brother Leonard Calvert—who would become the future governor of Maryland colony—deal firmly but courteously with Claiborne. It was made clear that Lord Baltimore believed that Kent Island lay fully within the boundaries of the Maryland charter, and while they would permit Claiborne to continue trading, it would have to be under license and authority of Lord Baltimore.

Once word of Baltimore's charter arrived in Virginia, the colony planters were enraged over the challenge to their borders and petitioned the king to redress the issue. The king, however, decided to let the colonists sort out the problem among themselves. It was a decision that would quickly result in charges of piracy, bloodshed, and the first naval engagement between English-speaking peoples in the New World.

Two small vessels carrying the first settlers for Lord Baltimore's new colony arrived at Point Comfort on the Chesapeake River on February 27, 1634. It was a dangerous landfall, as Baltimore had specifically forbidden entry at either Jamestown or Virginia's new fort at Point Comfort.

The Maryland colonists, however, were treated kindly by Virginia's governor, John Harvey, despite the outright hostility of the Virginia Council. Governor Harvey seemed eager to lay aside the challenge to Virginia's territorial jurisdiction and assist Maryland's colonists. As a practiced politician, he obviously was motivated more by a desire for personal gain than simple neighborliness. It seems that Harvey had made an arrangement with Lord Baltimore to assist the colonists; in exchange, he would "receive a great summe of money due to him out of the exchequer."

On Kent Island, William Claiborne requested the Virginia Council's opinion as to "how he should demean himself in respect to Lord Baltimore's patent and his deputies, now seated in the bay; for that they [the Marylanders] had specified . . . that he was now a member of that plantation, and therefore should relinquish all relations and dependence on this colony." The council, quite possibly in opposition to the will of their own governor, stoutly reassured him that Kent Island remained part of the Virginia colony.

Each colony seemed equally adamant in its claim to the island, so Claiborne decided to take matters into his own hands. Having served as both the secretary of state for Virginia and a member of the Virginia Council, he decided to oppose the king's charter and resist Lord Baltimore's claim over Kent Island. It was with this decision that Claiborne's real troubles began.

Maryland's colonists began establishing the settlement of St. Mary's City on a bluff overlooking a tributary of the Potomac they dubbed St. Mary's River. They initially secured the friendship of the local Algonquin Indians, but by the summer of 1643, suspicion, distrust, and periodic hostilities were increasingly evident among the neighboring Patuxent tribe. Alarmed by this change in local attitude toward their presence, the settlers of St. Mary's abandoned their domestic projects and set about building defenses. A Virginia fur trader named Henry Fleet informed the Maryland colonists that their neighbor William Claiborne was spreading rumors among the Indians that the new settlers were "Waspaines," or Spaniards intent on murdering the local tribes.

The Maryland settlers were outraged and immediately made a formal complaint to Virginia governor John Harvey, who had Claiborne placed under bond and confined to Jamestown under the watchful custody of Captains Samuel Matthews and John Utie until the charges could be investigated. On June 20, 1634, commissioners from both Maryland and Virginia, along with Claiborne, met with the Indians at their village on the Patuxent River. As a consequence of the meeting, not only was William Claiborne fully vindicated of the charge of turning the Indians against the Marylanders, but it also became apparent that Henry Fleet had started the rumor because he was jealous of Claiborne's success.

Meanwhile, Claiborne's partners, William Cloberry and Company, had petitioned King Charles to protect their claims on Kent Island. The king replied that dispossessing the Kent Islanders was contrary to justice and the intent of the colonial charter granted to the Calverts. Furthermore, he directed that the islanders should continue to enjoy full freedom of trade and instructed Lord Baltimore not to disturb or molest the settlement in any way.

That should have been the end of it, but it wasn't. In September, news of the king's command and the charges against Claiborne both reached Lord Baltimore—but not the news that Claiborne had been exonerated of all charges. Based on this incomplete information, Baltimore became outraged. Ignoring the king's admonition to the contrary, he sent word to his brother, Governor Calvert, that if Claiborne continued to trade without an official Maryland license, he was to be arrested and held in jail at St. Mary's, and his island settlement confiscated. But arresting the secretary of state of a more powerful and better established neighboring colony was not a simple matter. So Lord Baltimore used his connections at court to bring pressure on Virginia's governor to promise full support to Maryland in its claims. Opposition to both Governor Harvey and Maryland colony was spreading through Virginia, and trade and commerce between the two colonies virtually ceased.

William Claiborne resolved to stand fast in spite of his own governor's support of Lord Baltimore. He prepared Kent Island for armed resistance while simultaneously expanding operations. He imported more servants, cleared more land, and erected more houses. His partner, William Cloberry, reassured by the king's support, sent new shiploads of goods to trade with the Indians.

When the Europeans' squabbling over Kent Island became unbearable to the indigenous Indians, the Susquehannock and Wicomese tribes raided the island and killed three settlers before being repelled. After the attack, the islanders erected two more fortifications and Claiborne commissioned the construction of a lightweight ship, known as a "pinnace." Named the *Long Tayle*, it was designed for naval defense as well as for trade and transport. Once complete, Claiborne put the *Long Tayle* and her crew of twenty men under the command of Captain Thomas Smith.

The flashpoint for the escalating hostilities between St. Mary's and Kent Island came when another pinnace belonging to Maryland, commanded by Sergeant Robert Vaughn, approached Garrett Island near the head of the Chesapeake with a cargo destined for the Indian trade. The historical record is unclear as to how the altercation started or exactly what transpired, but a man named John Butler, agent for and brother-in-law of William Claiborne, seized the Maryland ship, its cargo, Sergeant Vaughn, and the rest of the crew. The prisoners were taken to Kent Island. This seizure was the first documented act of "Pyracie" on the waters of the Chesapeake Bay. Claiborne ordered Vaughn and company released, but with the understanding that they would carry word back to St. Mary's of his resolve to resist any incursion on the part of the Marylanders. He then continued in his trading activities as though nothing had happened. On April 5, Captain Smith sailed the *Long Tayle* on a trading mission to the Indian village at Mattapany, on the shores of the Patuxent River in St. Mary's County. In retaliation for the earlier capture, two Maryland captains seized the *Long Tayle* and ordered Captain Smith to produce a valid trading license from Lord Baltimore. Smith could not produce the demanded license, but he did produce a copy of the king's commission and additional correspondence confirming it. The Marylanders declared the documents fakes and proceeded to confiscate the vessel and its cargo. They did, however, release Captain Smith. Apparently, they wanted it well known that Maryland would not tolerate any incursion into its territory.

The Kent Islanders were enraged by the capture of their only ship and plotted their revenge. They fitted out and armed a sloop named the *Cockatrice,* manning it with a crew of fourteen. Claiborne issued a special warrant to Lieutenant Ratcliffe Warren to seize any vessel belonging to Maryland. It was a warrant that was—depending on one's point of view—either a declaration of war or a letter of marque for privateering. Governor Calvert, fearing the escalating hostilities, armed and readied two vessels of his own, the *St. Helen* and *St. Margaret,* and placed them under the command of his most trusted officers, Captain Thomas Cornwaleys and Cuthbert Fenwick.

Just two weeks after the confiscation of the *Long Tayle,* while cruising in the Pocomoke River on Virginia's lower eastern shore, Lieutenant Warren sighted the *St. Helen* and moved to take the ship. Just as the *Cockatrice* cruised into range, its crew was surprised by the arrival of the *St. Margaret,* commanded by Captain Cornwaleys. Undaunted, the Kent Islanders shifted direction, closed, and attempted to board the *St. Margaret.* A short, brutal hand-to-hand battle ensued, resulting in the deaths of Warren, two other Kent Islanders and one member of the *St. Margaret's* crew. Several crewmen on both sides were wounded, and the *Cockatrice* was captured. The first blood of naval combat on the Chesapeake Bay had been spilled. It would be far from the last.

For William Claiborne, the loss of the *Cockatrice* was devastating, but he dispatched another armed vessel under the command of Captain Thomas Smith to patrol the mouth of the Pocomoke. On May 10, Smith encountered Cornwaleys's ship in the harbor of the Great Wicomico. Though details of the engagement were never recorded, the Kent Islanders apparently emerged victorious, as Cornwaleys's corn, furs, trading goods, and possibly his ship were captured. They had settled the score for the loss and capture of the *Cockatrice*. Claiborne next sent Captain Philip Taylor in another vessel up the Patuxent to retake the *Long Tayle*, but once again the tables were turned, and Captain Taylor was taken.

While his "privateers" were waging recurring battles on the Pocomoke, William Claiborne was at Jamestown garnering support against Governor Harvey. Maryland's Governor Calvert demanded that the Virginia governor surrender Claiborne for trial, but the increasingly unpopular Harvey was facing open insurrection because of his support for the Marylanders' claim on Kent Island and found himself unable to comply with the demands of his northern neighbors. In fact, Harvey was impeached and sent to England to face charges. In his place, the Virginia Council elected Captain John West to act as governor and broker an uneasy truce between the Marylanders and the Kent Islanders.

Then a man named George Evelin arrived on the scene. When Evelin came to Kent Island in December 1636 with a one-sixth share in Cloberry and Company, he seemed a welcome asset. But when the first shipment of supplies and trade goods arrived a couple months later, the islanders learned that Evelin had managed to acquire power of attorney through Cloberry, and now declared that he had been granted command of Kent Island and full control of its operations. William Claiborne was ordered to return to England to explain his actions against Lord Baltimore. Claiborne dutifully made preparations for his voyage, but before he left, he made rapid progress on a permanent plantation and trading center under the command of Captain Thomas Smith on Palmer's Island, strategically located at the head of the bay and in the heart of Maryland territory. He also prepared an inventory of company property and made Evelin sign a bond agreeing not to sell or assign Kent Island or its goods.

As soon as Claiborne disappeared over the horizon Evelin broke the bond and began personal negotiations with Maryland's governor. Courted, flattered, and likely bribed by Governor Calvert, Evelin soon transferred his allegiance from Cloberry and Company to Lord Baltimore. Calvert instructed him to secure the goodwill of the Kent Islanders in support of Lord Baltimore; in exchange, the governor would appoint him commander of Kent Island and he would receive a share in all proceeds from it.

The Kent Islanders, however, viewing Evelin as both traitor and turncoat, were loath to transfer their allegiance, despite the best efforts of their new commander. Trade deteriorated and the Marylanders severed the supply lines. The threat of starvation was growing among the islanders, who almost universally despised Evelin. Two of Claiborne's most trusted and loyal agents, John Butler and Thomas Smith, led the islanders in resisting Evelin and they became marked men among Maryland officials.

Governor Calvert, whose past efforts against Kent Island had not fared well, was reluctant to employ force to reinstall Evelin without clear instructions from his brother, Lord Baltimore, who remained safely back in England. In the late autumn of 1637, however, news reached Maryland that an attack by Susquehannock Indians was likely. Fearing that the Virginians might supply the Indians with guns and gunpowder via the trading post at Palmer's Island, the Marylanders decided that both Kent and Palmer's Islands would have to be taken by force. Calvert gathered a force of roughly thirty musketeers under the command of Cornwaleys, which moved out with George Evelin in tow. Meanwhile, the Kent Islanders heard about the Marylanders' fear of an Indian attack and decided it might actually be a good idea to supply and encourage the Susquehannocks while simultaneously fortifying Palmer's Island.

In February 1638, Marylanders landed at the southernmost point of Kent Island near Captain Claiborne's house, which was "seated within a small fort of Pallysadoes." The Marylanders took the lightly defended fort by surprise and without opposition. Claiborne was still in England, and a thorough search failed to turn up Butler or Smith, "the chief incendiaries of the former seditions and mutinies upon the island." Undeterred, Governor Calvert rounded up everyone in the fort and set off on a march toward Butler's plantation, five miles to the north. He directed his ship to rendezvous with them at Craford, Evelin's headquarters on the island. When the Marylanders came within half a mile of Butler's plantation, Calvert dispatched an ensign named Clerck with ten musketeers to surprise and capture Butler and bring him to Craford. He next dispatched his sergeant, Robert Vaughn, along with six musketeers, to Thomas Smith's plantation at Beaver Neck, located on the far side of a small creek. They captured both Butler and Smith and confined them aboard the pinnace on charges of piracy.

Having captured the leaders of the opposition, Governor Calvert issued a proclamation of general pardon to any remaining Kent Islanders who submitted to Lord Baltimore's government within twenty-four hours. Not surprisingly, this is precisely what all the residents of Kent Island did. Calvert then directed that the islanders would have to accept Lord Baltimore's letters patent for their holdings on the island, telling them that new boundaries would be surveyed in the spring. Calvert sailed back to St. Mary's with Smith and Butler under heavy guard, leaving Evelin in command of Kent Island.

Once he arrived at St. Mary's, Calvert faced the vexing question of what to do with Butler and Smith. In an effort to win him over, Calvert brought Butler out of the sheriff's custody and into his own home. If he could manage to secure Butler's support, he hoped, the rest of Kent Island might follow suit. Smith, on the other hand, had commanded two of Claiborne's ships and was responsible for the death of William Ashmore at the Battle of Pocomoke, as it had come to be called. Calvert needed to make an example of Smith. In March 1638, Smith was indicted, found guilty, and sentenced to hang for piracy and murder.

As a show of mercy and clemency, however, Governor Calvert issued a stay of execution and released Smith on bail, hoping he had made his point and demonstrated his authority. But once free on bail, Smith returned to Kent Island, where he immediately set about raising a revolt against Maryland.

Infuriated, Calvert fitted out a second expedition and returned to the troublesome island with fifty musketeers. They reinforced the Kent Island fort with several cannons and removed all of Cloberry's goods and servants. The Marylanders once again captured Smith and took him to St. Mary's under guard. This time, though, there would be no mercy. He was hanged—not for piracy, but for rebellion.

Butler eventually converted to the Maryland cause and was appointed captain of the Militia Band of the Isle of Kent. Ironically, his commission included mustering inhabitants capable of bearing arms to repel pirate invasions and Indians, as well as suppressing mutiny and civil disorder.

Meanwhile, William Claiborne, whom the Maryland Assembly charged on March 24, 1638, with "grevious crimes of pyracie and murther" for the Battle of Pocomoke, became a wanted criminal and outlaw in the Maryland colony. Consequently, he forfeited all of "his lands and tenements" as well as his "goods and chattels which he hath within this Province" to Lord Baltimore.

Naturally, Claiborne petitioned the king, but the Crown wanted nothing more to do with the quarrelsome colonies and referred the matter to the Lords Commissioners of Plantations. In April 1638, the Lords Commissioners predictably ruled in favor of their fellow peer, Lord Baltimore. Baltimore's power and influence in England was simply too great to fight.

With such powerful political forces standing firmly behind Maryland, and with both Kent and Palmer's Islands under the control of Governor Calvert, Virginia withdrew all support from William Claiborne. And the islands became a permanent part of Maryland.

Richard Ingle

In the long, rich history of Maryland piracy, there is one name that appears over and over again: Captain Richard Ingle. Ingle has variously been referred to as a "pirate," a "rebel," an "ungrateful villain," and a host of other, equally unflattering names. But "truth" has a way of becoming subjective and, as so often happens when historical fact blurs with legend, many accounts of Ingle and his exploits were written by individuals who relied as much on rumor and legend as on the historical record. So let us try to uncover the facts in the very strange case of Captain Richard Ingle. Mixed in with Ingle's bizarre story are many incidents and individuals that we encountered in the previous chapter, proving that history, like real life, is never as clean-cut as we might like it to be.

Between 1642 and 1651, England was fractured by a terrible civil war that pitted King Charles I and the Catholics and progressive Protestants who backed him against the radically fundamentalist Protestants known as "Puritans" and "Roundheads," who controlled Parliament. The war would eventually end with the beheading of King Charles and the imposition of more than a decade of draconian rule under Oliver Cromwell and the Parliamentarian party.

Surprising as it may seem, at least a part of the war was fought far across the Atlantic Ocean, in Maryland Colony. In 1632, King Charles granted a vast tract of land to Cecilius Calvert, Second Lord Baltimore, a liberal Catholic who envisioned his new colony as a place where people of all religions could turn their back on the religious turmoil of Europe and live together in peace. To express his gratitude, Baltimore named the new colony Marie's Land in honor of King Charles's wife, Henrietta Maria, who was also a Catholic.

Only later would the name of the colony be shortened from Marie's Land to Maryland.

Maryland was chartered as a "palatinate" colony, with Lord Baltimore serving as its designated Lord Protector and liaison between the king and the colony; in effect, Baltimore served as a sub-king, acting in Charles's name in all things. Settlers in the new colony enjoyed all the rights of other Englishmen except for the fact that Lord Baltimore technically owned all of the land and collected all rents, taxes, and fees. He was also granted absolute political power and judicial authority and could order the construction of fortifications, confer honors and titles, distribute land grants, incorporate boroughs and towns, and license trade. He was also the nominal head of the church in Maryland. Despite holding so much power, Baltimore seems to have been a fair man and his people seem to have liked him. The problem did not lie in Maryland at all, but in the neighboring colony of Virginia.

Lord Baltimore and his charter were not well thought of in Virginia Colony because most of what was now Maryland had been included in the original charter that established Virginia. At least as bad as the fact that much of Maryland had been "stolen" from Virginia was the fact that Baltimore was a Catholic and he insisted on being tolerant to other Catholics and inviting them to his colony. Considering the religious factionalism that was about to start tearing England apart, it was inevitable that the hatred and bigotry that was so rampant in the mother country would spill over into the colonies.

Richard Ingle was a tobacco trader who sailed up and down the Chesapeake, collecting and selling tobacco on behalf of local growers; he was also a fanatical Puritan who named his ship *Reformation*. His opinion of Catholics was low and, like most Puritans and nearly all of the English Parliament, he hated King Charles, who he saw as being "soft" on Catholics and who even had the temerity to take a Catholic woman as his wife. Unlike most Puritans, however, Ingle did not have the sense to keep a civil tongue in his head. In February 1642, while in Accomac, Virginia, he made what were referred to as "treasonable remarks" against the King. But this was Protestant Virginia and the King was generally held in pretty low regard, so nothing happened. A year later, in March or April of 1643, Ingle repeated his slanderous remarks while his boat was moored along the Maryland coast. Although many of the Catholic locals were obviously shocked and scandalized, Lord Calvert did not move to have Ingle arrested or detained for questioning. By the beginning of the following year, however, Lord Calvert had retired as governor, and on January 18, 1644, his interim successor, Giles Brent, issued a warrant for the arrest of Richard Ingle on charges of high treason. The warrant was passed to a man named William Hardige with authorization to execute the arrest. Assigned to help Hardige was Captain Thomas Cornwalyes, a member of the St. Mary's council.

Amazingly, Ingle was arrested and taken into custody on the same day the arrest order was issued. Capturing Ingle may have been easy, but holding him proved to be a bit harder. Two days later, on January 20, he escaped and sailed to Kent Island, whose own peculiar problems and questionable political allegiances we looked at in the last chapter. In response to Ingle's escape, Governor Brent issued the following warrant to the local sheriff:

> I do hereby require (in His Majesty's name) Richard Ingle, mariner, to yield his body to Rob Ellyson, Sheriff of the County, before the first of February next, to answer such crimes of treason, as on his Majesty's behalf shall be objected against him, upon his utmost peril, of the law in that behalf. And I do further require all persons that can say or disclose any matter of treason against the said Richard Ingle to inform his Lordship's Attorney of it sometime before the said Court to the end it may be then & there prosecuted.

On January 29, Hardige and others were summoned to appear before the Maryland Council to give evidence of "pyratical & treasonable offences" in the case of Richard Ingle. For the first time, charges of piracy had been formally leveled against Ingle. While Ingle had not been rearrested we know he was still in the immediate vicinity because on January 30 the *Reformation* was seen riding at anchor in the St. George River and there were several accounts of

Ingle having been seen in the area. Over the course of the next week Governor Brent held four separate public inquests into Ingle and his activities and each returned the verdict of *ignoramus,* meaning insufficient evidence. It could well be that the public's lack of knowledge about Ingle and his doings were directly linked to the fact that he was the largest tobacco shipper in the area and without him and the *Reformation* the planters along the Chesapeake would have found it difficult to get their product to England.

The inquests' findings did not please Governor Brent, who immediately issued another warrant accusing Ingle of having committed an assault on the "vessels, guns, goods and person" of a man named only as "Bishop." Specifically, Ingle was said to have committed "the said crimes of pyracie, mutinie, tresspasse, contempt & misdemeanors & every of them severally." The charges may have been vague but they were certainly all-encompassing. Still, Ingle remained on the loose and no one seemed willing to testify against him. Largely due to the lack of evidence against Ingle, Captain Cornwaleys, who may have known Ingle and seems to have been sympathetic to him, managed to broker an agreement with the governor whereby Ingle agreed to appear in court no later than February 8 of the following year to answer the charges against him. In the meantime he could remain free if he posted a bond of one barrel of gunpowder and 400 pounds of lead shot. Considering the fact that the charges of treason and piracy which had been brought against Ingle carried the death penalty, it was an astounding change in policy. Still, Ingle would not comply with the bond order and Brent again ordered his arrest.

This time Richard Ingle did not escape the long arm of the law. He was arrested and turned over to the sheriff, and his ship was impounded until such time as Ingle either cleared himself of the multifarious charges levied against him or was found guilty—in which case he would certainly have no further use for a ship. With the *Reformation* lying at anchor, Governor Brent ordered the following proclamation to be nailed to its mainmast:

These are to publish & proclaim to all persons as well seamen as others, that Richard Ingle, master of this ship, is arrested upon high treason to his Majesty, & therefore to require all persons to aiding and assisting to his Lordships' officers in the seizing of his ship, & not to offer any resistance or contempt hereunto, not be any otherwise aiding or assisting to the said Richard Ingle upon peril of high treason to his Majesty.

Despite these strong words there were still individuals willing to come to Ingle's aid, and Captain Cornwaleys was still among them. But arranging a bond is one thing; breaking an accused pirate out of jail is quite another. Because the town of St. Mary's did not have a jail, the county sheriff, Edward Parker, was obliged to keep personal guard over his prisoner. When council members Thomas Cornwaleys, John Hampton, and James Neale told Sheriff Parker that Governor Brent and the council had authorized them to take Ingle to his ship for some reason, Parker could not object, but he insisted that he would have to go along. When Cornwaleys, Neale, Hampton, Parker, and Ingle reached the *Reformation*, Cornwaleys convinced Parker that he should give his guards a break and allow them to go ashore. Parker agreed; shortly after his men left, Ingle's crew climbed aboard the ship, ejected the sheriff, Cornwaleys, and his friends, and sailed away. How complicit Neal and Hampton were in the proceedings is unknown, but all of them, including Sheriff Parker and Captain Cornwaleys, were impeached on charges of being accessories to high treason.

Evidence as to exactly who knew how much was so scant that Parker, Hampton, and Neale were allowed to go free after losing their official positions, but since someone had to pay, Cornwaleys bore the brunt of official guilt. In addition to having to pay the largest fine that the law allowed, he was fined an additional one thousand pounds of tobacco. No longer welcome in polite society, Cornwaleys slipped out of Maryland and into Virginia where he waited sullenly for the return of his friend, Richard Ingle.

In late February 1644, less than six weeks after the entire affair began, Richard Ingle returned to St. Mary's, unloaded a cargo of goods, and took on a cargo of tobacco, which he intended to take to England. In April the *Reformation* set sail from Accomac, Virginia, for her transatlantic crossing; on board with Ingle and his load of tobacco was Thomas Cornwaleys.

During the summer of 1644, England was not a happy place. Long-running battles between the Crown and Parliament were violent, bloody, and indecisive, and neither side seemed to be gaining any advantage over the other. In an attempt to gather help wherever they could find it, both sides issued letters of marque to any American captain or ship owner willing to plunder the other sides' ships. While England teetered on the brink of anarchy, Maryland's new governor, Leonard Calvert (the younger brother of Lord Baltimore), sailed from Bristol to take up his position in St. Mary's City. In Calvert's luggage was a royal commission instructing him to capture any and all ships sailing on the Chesapeake whose owners supported the Parliamentarian cause. As soon as he reached the New World, Calvert met with his Virginia counterparts who, although sworn to uphold the king's cause, refused to cooperate because seizing parliamentary privateers might damage their tobacco trade. Virginians cared little who won the war in England, but they cared very much about getting their tobacco to market.

While Maryland and Virginia argued the merits of political loyalty over profit, the English Parliament issued a letter of marque to Richard Ingle and the *Reformation*, licensing them to take ships loyal to the Crown in either English or American waters or on the open sea. Ingle sailed from London in October 1644 with a hold full of cargo and a license to attack the Crown's ships. Shortly after the first of December 1644, he arrived safely in Virginia.

Less than two weeks after Ingle landed, William Claiborne—the former head of the Kent Island settlement and now a member of the Virginia Council, whom we met in the previous chapter—mounted an armed invasion of St. Mary's City and drove Governor Calvert out of the colony, forcing him to seek exile in Virginia. Having no intention of being driven from his job and his brother's colony, Calvert hired two spies and sent them to Kent Island three days before Christmas with instructions to find out everything they could about Claiborne's plans and the size of his militia. On New Year's Day 1645, Calvert declared William Claiborne to be "an enemy of the Province" and gave William Braithwaite the title of Commander of Kent Island and told him to raise whatever force he needed to seize the island and take control of it.

Calvert now had two enemies, both of whom were determined to keep him out of Maryland, and each of whom wanted control of the colony for himself. For the next fourteen months Maryland was wracked by raids, attacks, and counterattacks, and anarchy reached near totality as the three warring factions attacked one another's positions. There is no evidence that Richard Ingle and William Claiborne ever worked in concert—or, on the other hand, that they ever attacked each other—but their combined attacks nearly brought Maryland to its knees. The only difference between the two was that Ingle professed to be working for Parliament and Claiborne said he was working for Virginia. Anywhere Claiborne was not harassing the people of Maryland, Ingle was.

Ingle's band of thugs robbed and raided indiscriminately, capturing Catholic priests and shipping them to England to stand trial. On St. Valentine's Day 1645, Richard Ingle's *Reformation* and another ship sailed up the St. George River to St. Inigoes Creek, where they attacked and seized the trading ship *Der Spiegel* (The Mirror), which was registered in the neutral country of Holland. While sacking the ship they took as prisoner one of the passengers, Giles Brent, former acting governor of Maryland and the man who had made Ingle's life so very difficult. Only hours after taking *Der Spiegel* and making it a secondary pirate ship, Ingle landed an armed force of indeterminate size and overran St. Mary's City, which he promptly claimed in the name of Parliament. Soon thereafter Ingle attempted to capture the *Trewlove*, a small pinnace from Bristol, England, which had just arrived in America. The *Trewlove* was about one mile up St. Inigoes Creek when the *Reformation* spotted it. The shallow-drafted *Trewlove* made for shallow waters where the larger *Reformation* could not follow and eventually escaped under the cover of night.

Possibly out of sheer frustration over the loss of the *Trewlove*, Ingle sent seven of his men ashore the next morning with instructions to seize Cross House, the largest and finest home in all of Maryland Colony. While such a rich prize may appear to have been an obvious target for Ingle, it should be pointed out that Cross House was the home of Thomas Cornwaleys, Ingle's supporter and rescuer. Far truer to his violent nature than to his friends, Ingle had his men drive Cornwaleys' wife from her home before sacking and pillaging it to the point that it was a complete ruin. His excuse was that he didn't want the house to be fortified by the Catholics for use as a garrison.

Not content with robbing friends and strangers alike, Ingle now took to kidnapping individuals who he knew to be plotting against him. Included on Ingle's "enemies list" were Maryland secretary John Lewgar, a Jesuit priest named Thomas Copley, and, not surprisingly, Governor Leonard Calvert, who was now in exile in Virginia. Giles Brent would have been on the list, but he was already in Ingle's custody. While Ingle ran rampant across Maryland, Calvert was laying plans to raise a militia force composed predominantly of Catholics. Although greatly outnumbered by Protestants loyal to Parliament, Calvert's militia managed to gain a large enough foothold on Maryland soil to construct a fort. The Protestants countered by building a fort of their own and the situation again deteriorated into a series of raids and foraging expeditions that inevitably left homes, farmsteads, and villages devastated.

One facet of Ingle's bizarre master plan was a plot to capture as many Roman Catholic priests as possible and take them to England in chains. He believed that by parading the captured clergymen before the rabidly puritanical Parliament he would be able to prove that there was a Catholic plot to take over all of the colonies and that this would, somehow, relieve him of any guilt for the havoc he had caused in Maryland. Toward this end, Ingle plundered several small Catholic missions, burning their chapels and the homes of the priests. During the course of these raids Father Thomas Copley—one of the people on Ingle's enemies list—and a priest named Andrew White were taken prisoner and at least three other, unnamed Jesuit monks simply disappeared. Their fate can only be guessed at.

Ingle's pursuit of Governor Calvert was no less intense than his quest for Catholic clergymen, but it was notably less successful. After repeated failed attempts to capture Calvert, by mid-March of 1645 Ingle settled on carrying out a series of devastating raids on Kent Island, stealing anything he could carry away and burning everything else. By the end of the month the holds of both the *Reformation* and *Der Spiegel* were full to bursting with plundered loot and tobacco, and shortly after the first of April Ingle set sail for England. In addition to his booty, the hold of *Reformation* held four Catholic prisoners: Giles Brent, Secretary John Lewgar, and Fathers Thomas Copley and Andrew White. The *Reformation* and *Der Spiegel* reached London in early June 1645. What followed was not only a far cry from what Richard Ingle must have imagined, but certainly counts as one of the most bizarre sequences of events in maritime history.

Within days of landing, Ingle filed a lawsuit against the Dutch owners of *Der Spiegel* "for trading with a port hostile to Parliament." If suing the rightful owners of a ship which you had stolen seems odd, it was no less so than what followed. Two weeks after Ingle filed his suit, Thomas Cornwaleys, who had now been in exile in England for more than a year, sued Ingle for destroying his house in Maryland. To make matters worse, Parliamentarian authorities refused to accept any of Ingle's hostages as prisoners and both former governor Giles Brent and Father Copley sued Ingle for seizure of their property and false imprisonment. In November 1645, Richard Ingle countersued *everybody.* The list of suits and countersuits is mind-boggling and we will make no attempt to list them here. Suffice it to say that while Ingle may have insisted he was only supporting Parliament, the courts had no sympathy for him. For nearly two and a half years, the trials dragged on, and by September 1647 everything that Richard Ingle had stolen, including *Der Spiegel,* along with the only thing that was rightfully his, the *Reformation,* had been taken by the courts and handed over to his victims in compensation for their losses. Having lost everything, Richard Ingle was never able to return to America and simply disappeared from history.

Back in Maryland, Governor Leonard Calvert's militia band found retaking Maryland easier when they only had to fight the forces of one enemy, William Claiborne. By the summer of 1646,

Governor Leonard Calvert had returned to Maryland and reclaimed St. Mary's City in the name of his brother and the Crown. Over the next few months the last of Claiborne's men were rounded up or killed and, after nearly two years of violence and anarchy, peace—or a relative semblance of peace—descended on Maryland.

Roger Makeele

In his 1916 book about manor houses on the Eastern Shore, Swepson Earle remarked that "tradition says [Watts Creek, south of Denton] once provided refuge for Captain Kidd, whose 'buried treasure' has been sought on its banks."

Like so many other storytellers, Earle thoroughly confused his pirate legends. A generation later in the 1940s, Hulbert Footner related in his book, *Rivers of the Eastern Shore*, this story about Blackbeard:

> We set out from Cambridge and, during the drive south, my companion [a waterman from Cambridge] entertained me with tall tales of the rivers. We had been talking about the deep, unexpected holes that are to be found in all Eastern Shore rivers, due to some obscure action of the tides. My friend said, with a perfectly grave face:
>
> "There is such a hole near the mouth of Watts Creek that is ninety feet deep. It is called Jake's Hole. Its exact depth is known because it's been sounded often enough, and I'll tell you why. There was aplenty pirates round here in the old time. The one that mostly cruised in these waters was Blackbeard; Edward Teach was his right name. Well, Blackbeard picked Jake's Hole for one of his caches, and dropped an oaken chest bound round with copper bands in there. It's still there. God knows what's inside it!
>
> "Many knew about this and aimed to recover the treasure, but Blackbeard had left a school of man-eating red herring to guard the place and none could come near. Well, there was an Englishman called Lord Longbow bought a fine place on

the river and his cousin, Prince Fakir, came to spend the summer with him. Lord Longbow took him out in a boat to show him the river, and as they passed by Jake's Hole he was trying to teach Prince Fakir to sing "Yankee Doodle." This tickled the man-eating red herring so that they laughed theirselves to death.

"Those that knew about it thought it would be a cinch, then, to recover Blackbeard's treasure, so they proceeded to Jake's Hole with their ropes and grappling irons and so forth. But it turned out that Blackbeard had left another spell on the chest. It was easy enough to catch holt of it, but as soon as they hoisted it near the surface, the ropes bust into flame and burned through with an awful stink of sulphur, and the chest dropped to the bottom of the hole again. Many have tried it, but it was always the same. They only lost their grappling irons for their trouble. So the chest is there yet, if you want to have a try for it.

"That famous beard of his," the storyteller continued, "started growing right under his eyes and would have hung down over his chest, only he used to plait it in many little tails which he tied with different colored ribbons and caught behind his ears. I suppose you've heard how Blackbeard came to his end?"

I said I had not.

"Well, that was off Sharp's Island out in the bay. Blackbeard was lying in wait under the island at the edge of Dick's Hole for a richly laden Fast Indiaman that was expected down from Baltimore. He was so intent upon it, he failed to notice the tops'l schooner Julia Harlaw lying inside the hook. Young Joshua Covey was her master. Covey was able to creep up on Blackbeard in a yawl boat, and to board him before he was discovered. Covey cut off Blackbeard's head with one mighty sweep of his saber.

"But a pirate, you know, prided himself on never losing his head. Blackbeard threw the copper plate that showed the location of all his caches into Dick's Hole and jumped in after it. He swam around the vessel three times without his head before he disappeared from sight."

From the frequency with which one meets with his name on the Atlantic Coast, one would think that Blackbeard must have sailed from the Florida Keys to Nova Scotia, but it has been established that he never sailed north of Philadelphia. He laid such a spell of horror up and down the whole Atlantic seaboard that the appearance of any pirate would eventually be credited to the terrible Mr. Teach.

The Watts Creek pirate legends may have been attributed to Blackbeard, but they probably began with the true stories of a real Chesapeake pirate: Roger Makeele and his band from Tangier Sound. The activities of Roger Makeele and his band of pirates are known from the testimony of their victims, and colonial warrants for their arrest, as recorded in the Maryland and Virginia archives.

Makeele first appears in the Maryland records in January 1685, at the dawn of the golden age of piracy. Makeele and a small band of thugs, including three from the "Jenckins plantation" on Watts Island, assaulted the crew of a small tobacco-laden sloop. The crew had put the vessel into an inlet on Watts Island and were sitting by their fire when Makeele and his men attacked under the cover of darkness. The pirates seized the sloop, kidnapped the crew, and deposited them in marshes on the mainland of Dorchester County. The captain of the crew recognized Makeele and denounced him before the Maryland authorities.

Makeele and his band attempted to seize another vessel two weeks later—this time by trying to lure the crew to their camp on Watts Island. The crew were warned by the captain of a nearby vessel, who reported that he "well knew said Makeele, and perceiving his designe to betray the strangers on shoare, took opportunity to acquaint them of the danger, and practice of said Roger . . . whereupon they repaired on board, and gott to Sayle."

Makeele's pirates became bolder and more active as the winter progressed. They not only attacked vessels on the bay but also stole goods from Native Americans on the Eastern Shore, and from settlers' homes on the Western Shore.

In February, authorities at St. Mary's City finally issued warrants
for the arrest of Makeele and his gang. In March, the governor of
Virginia ordered the ketch *Quaker* and two sloops, under the command of a Captain Allen, to "saile into ye bay and cruze about and
search all parts therein for ye aforesaid Roger Makeel and ye other of
his Complices."

Knowing that the law was actively hunting him, Makeele abandoned Watts Island as his base of operations and retreated to the
North Carolina Sounds, a well-known haven for local pirates. Virginia's governor requested law-enforcement assistance, but there is
no record that Carolina authorities (such as there were) responded.

Nobody knows what happened next. If Makeele returned to the
Chesapeake, he may have been arrested and executed. Perhaps Virginia's governor referred to him when he reported in late 1685 that
"some Pilfering Pyrates have done damage to the Inhabitants, but I
have taken the Chiefest and executed them."

After only a few months of piracy, Makeele was never mentioned
again in the colonial record. But the pirate legend of Watts Creek
still lives on to tantalize us more than three centuries later.

William Kidd

In April 1699, an important dispatch from the lords justice of England arrived in Virginia. The order directed the governor and council to be on the lookout for a buccaneer named William Kidd, who was commanding the ship *Adventure Galley*.

Countless books have been written about the life and exploits of the infamous Captain Kidd, and it is impossible to go into exhaustive detail about his adventures and misadventures here. But highlights of his career show that Kidd and his crew had a connection with the Maryland coast.

Kidd was born in Scotland around 1645. His father died when he was five years old, and the Kidd family immigrated to New York Colony. Kidd grew up in New York and apparently spent at least some time as a seaman's apprentice before beginning his own seafaring exploits.

The earliest surviving historical records for Kidd date from 1689, when he was about forty-four years old and a member of a pirate crew sailing in the Caribbean. Kidd and other members of the crew mutinied, ousted the captain of the ship, and sailed to the English colony of Nevis, where they renamed their confiscated ship the *Blessed William*.

Either by popular election among the crew or appointment by Christopher Codrington, governor of the island of Nevis, Kidd became captain of the *Blessed William* and his ship became part of a small fleet assembled by Codrington to defend Nevis from the French, with whom the English were at war. Governor Codrington had no money to pay the sailors for their services, so he told them they could take their pay from the French. And so the *Blessed William* became a privateering ship with letters of marque to attack any French ship or settlement. In due course, Kidd and his men attacked the French island of Mariegalante, destroyed and pillaged its only town, and confiscated a fortune in excess of two thousand pounds sterling.

Shortly after plundering Mariegalante, Kidd agreed to ally the *Blessed William* with the British Royal Navy in a major engagement against the French fleet. Many among Kidd's crew considered this a dangerous waste of time, since warships carried no treasure. The disagreement turned ugly and the men turned against their captain. Kidd tried to explain that they were working for the British and were therefore obligated to aid the Royal Navy, but his words fell on deaf ears. When Kidd rowed ashore while his ship was anchored at Nevis, the fractious crew stole the *Blessed William* and the loot stashed in its hold.

Governor Codrington courteously provided Kidd with a new ship and gave him permission to hunt down the mutineers. Kidd set out from Nevis, but once at sea he lost the *Blessed William*'s trail and eventually sailed to his hometown, New York City. Despite being a British colony, New York was, at the time, in open revolt against England. Loyal to the Crown, Kidd offered to carry guns and ammunition for British troops. In reward for his loyalty, the provincial assembly gave him 150 pounds sterling and lavish praises.

During his time in New York, Kidd met Sarah Bradley Cox Oort. Her second husband, John Oort, was a wealthy gentleman who owned several docks, as well as most of what is now Wall Street. Shortly after Kidd met Mrs. Oort, her husband died mysteriously; although no one has ever discovered the cause of Oort's death, some historians believe Kidd killed him, or at least speeded his passage into the next world—perhaps with the aid of Sarah. Suspiciously, only two days after Oort's demise, Kidd and the recently widowed Sarah applied for a marriage license.

Although William Kidd apparently loved his wife and her two daughters, he also profited from the marriage. According to the law of the day, Sarah's new husband gained control over all of her money and property, including her former husband's fortune, which she had inherited. At a single stroke, Kidd became a very rich man with land and shipping docks, a position among New York's wealthy elite, and thanks to the generosity of Governor Codrington, a ship called the *Antigua*. Although Kidd could have comfortably retired from the sea, he remained restless.

By the spring of 1695 he came up with a bold scheme. He would address the problem of marauding pirates who disrupted British shipping by sailing to pirate-infested waters and randomly taking pirates into custody. He would then "recover" the pirates' ill-gotten booty and divide it among his investors. With this slightly shady, convoluted plan in mind, he enlisted the support of Richard Coote, Earl of Bellomont and governor general of New York Colony, and Robert Livingston, an enterprising young Scot who had settled in New York City. Endorsed by the former and accompanied by the latter, Kidd visited London, where he formed a consortium to furnish the funds necessary to carry out his plan to plunder the plunderers.

King William III enthusiastically supported Kidd's scheme, partly because the pirates were strangling England's shipping and partly because he would receive a cut of the profits. The key, Kidd and Livingston knew, was to leave English ships untouched but hunt those of other countries—particularly Portugal, France, and Spain. This way they could enjoy a life of piracy and still be protected by the king of England. Besides Kidd, Livingston, and Coote, the venture eventually included the Duke of Shrewsbury, the Earls of Romney and Oxford, Sir Edmund Harrison, Lord Chancellor John Somers, and other notables. As foster father of the expedition, King William was to receive one-tenth of any proceeds.

The king granted Kidd two letters of marque. The first entitled him to apprehend "pirates, free-booters, and sea-rovers, being our subjects or of other nations associated with them," and to take pirates of any nationality—some of whom, like the notorious Thomas Tew, were specifically named—and authorized him to seize them and their vessels wherever he found them. If they resisted,

Kidd was authorized to use all necessary force in subduing them. The second letter of marque granted permission to take any ships belonging to France or its allies. Kidd's only limitation was that he was not allowed to attack English ships or those of England's allies.

By August 1696, the eight contributing partners purchased a ship, the *Adventure Galley*, for 6,000 pounds sterling. The noble lords, who were both investors and among the most powerful men in England, paid four-fifths of the cost of the ship and the voyage.

At over 284 tons, the *Adventure Galley* was well suited to the task of catching pirates; she carried thirty-two cannons, and although it was a rarity for warships of the time, she had forty-six sweeps (oars), which allowed the crew to row the ship when necessary. Under full sail, she could travel at a respectable fourteen knots; under oar, without wind, she could make three knots. The oars were a key advantage, because they allowed the ship to maneuver in battle when the wind died and other ships became immobilized.

Since the entire enterprise was speculative, the crew would sail without wages, their only pay being their share in any booty and prize money. Kidd and Livingston alone underwrote the expedition, agreeing to pay all expenses not met by its results. Should the ships take 100,000 pounds sterling or more in booty, Captain Kidd was to have the *Adventure Galley* given to him as a bonus. The success of the expedition rested entirely on seizing either French ships or pirates. Kidd's agreement with his backers stipulated that he had one year to hunt down prizes. If he failed to return with the promised booty by March 25, 1697, Captain Kidd would owe them 20,000 pounds sterling.

In April 1696, the *Adventure Galley* departed from England with a crew of about 140 men. As they sailed down the Thames, Kidd unaccountably failed to salute a Royal Navy vessel at Greenwich, as custom dictated. The navy ship fired a shot reminding him to show respect but in a shocking display of impudence, Kidd's crew reportedly responded by turning around and slapping their exposed backsides at the passing ship. The navy vessel retaliated by stopping the *Adventure Galley* and pressing many of her crewmen into service— not an auspicious beginning to the voyage.

Now shorthanded, Kidd continued toward New York, and still managed to capture a small French merchant vessel en route. To make up for his lack of men, Kidd picked up replacement crewmen in New York, the vast majority of whom were known to be hardened criminals, some undoubtedly former pirates. Governor Benjamin Fletcher of New York wrote to the Board of Trade about Kidd's crew: "Many flocked to him from all parts, men desperate of fortunes and necessities, in expectation of getting vast treasure. It is generally believed here that if he misses the design named in his commission, he will not be able to govern such a villainous herd."

On September 10, 1696, the men signed eighteen articles of agreement under which they would sail. The contract "between Capt. William Kidd Commander of the good ship *Adventure Galley* on the one part and John Walker Quarter Master to the said ships company on the other part," included the following stipulations:

That if any man shall lose an Eye, Legg or Arme or the use thereof . . . [he] shall receive . . . six hundred pieces of eight, or six able Slaves.

The man who shall first see a Sail. If she be a Prize shall receive one hundred pieces of eight.

That whosoever shall disobey Command shall lose his share or receive such Corporal punishment as the Capt. and Major part of the Company shall deem fit.

That man is proved a Coward in time of Engagement shall lose his share.

That man that shall be drunk in time of Engagement before the prisoners then taken be secured, shall lose his share.

That man that shall breed a Mutiny Riot on Board the ship or Prize taken shall lose his share and receive such Corporal punishment as the Capt. and major part of the Company shall deem fit.

That if any man shall defraud the Capt. or Company of any Treasure, as Money, Goods, Ware, Merchandizes or any other thing whatsoever to the value of one piece of eight . . .

[he] shall lose his Share and be put on shore upon the first inhabited Island or other place that the said ship shall touch at.

That what money or Treasure shall be taken by the said ship and Company shall be put on board the Man of War and there be shared immediately, and all Wares and Merchandizes when legally condemned to be legally divided amongst the ships Company according to Articles.

Although Kidd and his men were technically privateers, their articles of agreement were more akin to those signed by pirate corporations than those signed by sailors operating under letters of marque. Perhaps owing to the mutiny and theft of his ship and cargo earlier in his career, Kidd may have thought these articles a necessity to ensure that every man knew his place.

And so it was that in September 1696, Kidd weighed anchor and set course for the Cape of Good Hope at the southern tip of Africa. Although the wind and tides were with him, good fortune was not. Within a few weeks, a third of his crew were dead or dying of cholera, the newly built *Adventure Galley* was leaking, and worst of all, Kidd had failed to find any of the prizes he had expected to encounter off Madagascar. Now desperate, Kidd sailed northward to the Strait of Bab-el-Mandeb at the southern entrance of the Red Sea, a notorious pirate haunt. Again he failed to find any pirates. According to Edward Barlow, a captain employed by the British East India Company, Kidd attacked a Mughal convoy escorted by a British East Indiaman but he was driven off. If we are to believe this report, it marks Kidd's first foray into piracy while he was under the Crown's patronage.

As Kidd's enterprise slowly fell apart, he became more and more desperate to find a way of covering the costs of the expedition. The frustration must have taken a heavy toll on him, because on October 30, 1697, Kidd inadvertently killed one of his own crewmen. When a Dutch ship sailed into sight, Kidd's chief gunner, William Moore, urged Kidd to attack. But attacking a ship of England's ally would have been an act of piracy certain to anger England's Dutch-born King William III. Kidd refused, and a heated argument ensued. Infuriated, Kidd snatched up a bucket bound with iron hoops and struck Moore, fracturing his skull. Moore died the following day. Although seventeenth-century admiralty law afforded captains great latitude in the degree of violence they used to govern unruly crewmen, outright murder was not permitted. But Kidd seemed unconcerned, later explaining to his surgeon that he had "good friends in England" who would get him off the hook. Some of the crew deserted when the *Adventure Galley* next made port, and those who stayed behind voiced constant discontent and frequently made open threats of mutiny.

Despite the endless litany of problems, on January 30, 1698, Kidd took his greatest prize, the Armenian-owned *Quedagh Merchant*, loaded with an incredible variety of merchandise from India, including satins, silks, and muslins along with gold and silver. It was a rich bounty and a tremendous prize. Unfortunately, the captain of the *Quedagh Merchant*, a less-than-patriotic Englishman named Wright, had purchased passes from the French East India Company promising him the protection of the French Crown. After realizing that the captain of the taken vessel was an Englishman, Kidd tried to persuade his crew to return the ship to its owners. They refused, however, claiming that their prey was perfectly legal, as Kidd was commissioned to take French ships, and an Armenian ship counted as French if it had French passes. In an attempt to maintain his all-too-tenuous control over his crew, Kidd relented and kept the prize.

When news of the *Quedagh Merchant* incident reached England, it confirmed Kidd's reputation as a pirate, and various naval commanders were ordered to "pursue and seize the said Kidd and his accomplices" for the "notorious piracies" they had committed. Kidd kept the *Quedagh Merchant*'s French passes as well as the vessel herself. Although the passes offered only a dubious defense of his actions, British admiralty and vice admiralty courts, especially in North America, had often turned a blind eye at privateers' trespasses into piracy, and Kidd may have hoped that the passes would provide legal justification that would allow him to keep the *Quedagh*

Merchant and her cargo. Renaming the seized merchantman the *Adventure Prize*, he set sail for Madagascar.

Kidd finally reached Madagascar on April 1, 1698, and here he encountered the first actual pirate vessel of his voyage, the *Mocha Frigate*, captained by Robert Culliford—the same man who had stolen Kidd's ship, the *Blessed William*, years earlier. Two contradictory accounts exist of how Kidd reacted to this encounter.

According to one account, Kidd made peaceful overtures to Culliford: He "drank their Captain's health," swearing that "he was in every respect their Brother," and gave Culliford "a Present of an Anchor and some Guns." This account appears to be based on the later testimony of two of Kidd's crewmen. The other version contends that Kidd was unaware that Culliford had only about twenty crewmen and believed he was undermanned and ill equipped to take the *Mocha Frigate* until his two prize ships and crews arrived, so he decided not to molest Culliford until reinforcements came. After the *Adventure Prize* and *Rouparelle* appeared, Kidd ordered his crew to attack Culliford's *Mocha Frigate*. But his crew, despite their previous eagerness to seize any available prize, refused to attack Culliford and threatened to shoot Kidd. Whichever version of the encounter is true, two things are certain: Kidd failed to capture the *Mocha Frigate*—the only genuine pirate vessel he encountered in his expedition to hunt and capture pirates—and his crew was teetering on the brink of mutiny.

Kidd now resolved to return with his booty and prizes to New York, disband the current crew, divide the spoils, and refit the ships, but en route to New York, Kidd learned he had been declared a pirate and several English men-of-war were searching for him to claim the bounty on his head. Realizing that the *Adventure Prize* was a marked vessel, he disposed of it in the Caribbean and continued toward New York aboard a small sloop. He stopped at several places along the Virginia and Delaware coastline and secreted treasure away in various hiding places, hoping to use his knowledge of its location as a bargaining chip in the inevitable fight to clear his name and save his skin.

Back in England, the lords justice had, in compliance with the forceful persuasion of the immensely powerful East India Company, directed all colonial governors to apprehend Kidd and his associates in order that they might be "prosecuted to ye utmost rigor of law." If Kidd or any of his crew were apprehended in Virginia or Maryland, they were to be held until the king issued further commands.

Virginia governor Frances Nicholson dutifully directed all of the colony's militia commanders, sheriffs, customs agents, and naval officers to be on the alert and apprehend the pirates should they enter Old Dominion waters or make landfall anywhere along the coastline. A few days later, formal notices and proclamations were posted throughout Maryland and Virginia authorizing the capture of the pirates by any citizen.

After numerous false reports, false alarms, and a few false arrests, fears of pirate incursion only escalated once word arrived from the sheriff of Accomack County, Virginia, that Kidd had arrived on the coast. Apparently, the collector of customs for the Eastern Shore had told the sheriff that two ex-pirates named Stretcher and Lewis had informed him of Kidd's arrival. The two had been aboard Kidd's ship, which, they reported, boasted forty-two guns and was accompanied by an eighteen-gun sloop. The men claimed that at least 130 pirates were aboard the two vessels, although a handful of them had taken their leave; some were now en route to Philadelphia, with others shipping aboard a sloop belonging to Andrew Gravenrod and bound for Maryland. The pirates were heavily laden with plunder and booty, with their ships carrying "30 Tunns of Gold and Silver aboard," and the pair claimed that each of their company had a share equivalent to four thousand pounds sterling. In the government's view, the coastline lay under imminent threat and peril and one of the world's most wanted criminals was now within reach. Kidd, for his part, apparently felt secure on the waters of the Chesapeake: he reportedly sent word to his wife in New York to join him. But she never arrived.

Theophilus Turner, one of the men who left Kidd's ship in Delaware, boarded Andrew Gravenrod's sloop as she headed up the

Chesapeake, planning to take his treasure and settle quietly in the Tidewater area. While anchored in the Severn River, Gravenrod's sloop was visited by an agent of the Maryland governor. Turner was arrested, his treasure was confiscated, and he was forced to provide a deposition to the colonial governor. Turner's indictment had far less to do with his own complicit nature in the piratical crimes than with gathering evidence for use by Captain Kidd's political enemies.

The deposition of Theophilus Turner was sworn to Colonel Blakiston, governor of Maryland, on June 8, 1699, and documented Turner's transition from captured merchant seaman to pirate under command of Robert Culliford:

> That [Turner] sayled out of London about three years agoe in the Ship Hanniball, Captain William Hill Commander, which ship was a Merchant ship mounted with thirty two Gunns and Navigated with seventy Men, and went upon the Coast of Guinea, where the Captain put his Men to very short allowance so that severall of them, vizt. Henry Webber, 3d Mate, who afterwards Comanded the said ship, and severall others, took the ship from him and went to Brasile, where the Deponent [Turner] and some others left the ship. After that the Deponent had lived at Brasile about one yeare, a French Vessell which had lost her top mast arrived there under the Comand of Mounsieur de Ley, on Board of which Vessell the deponent embarqued himselfe for the Coast of India, the said De Ley being bound to Bengall, in the Voyage whereto they touched at the Island of Johannah, an Island [whose] inhabitants are Arabians, which was in the Month of May or June 1698: and riding there at Anchor with the said ship, came a ship of fourty Gunns called the Resolution by the Men on Board, But understood her right name was the Moco, [The *Mocha* had been a frigate belonging to the East India Company. Piratical members of the crew, led by James Gillam, had murdered the captain and had seized the ship.] from Madagaskar, Navigated with about 130 or 140 Men under the Comand of Captain Robert Culliford.

De Ley weighed one Anchor and cut the other Cable, but Culliford chasing him took him and brought the deponent on Board them, being the only Englishman on board De Ley, and examined him concerning Deleys Loading, with many threats. After they plundered the ship and found there 2000l. in money, besides Wine and Cloath, which they took, and because the Deponent was an Englishman they would not let him go on board De Ley again but kept him. After which the said Culliford sayled with the said ship upon the Coast of India: and about the middle of August came up with a Pyrate, who came out of America some where near Rhroad Island under the Comand of Richard Chivers, had 80 or 90 men and twelve Gunns, who kept Company and Consorted with Culliford. And about the End of September last they met off of Suratt with a turkey ship belonging to Suratt, which Chivers crew boarded: and the Quartermaster and some of Cullifords crew went on Board: she was laden with Pieces 8, Gold and Dollers, was reputed to the vallue of one Hundred and twenty or thirty thousand pounds. There were some shots made and several turks were killed and wounded and two or three of Chivers Company: they put the men on shoare on the Coast of India, sunck their own ship and took the turkey ship and then shared the money, about 700 or 800l. a man in each ship, and gave the Deponent who pumped for them on occasion and was ready at call, not deeming him as one of them but in the nature of a prisoner, and told him if that he would go out with them their next Voyage, he should be all one as the rest.

Enough evidence was gathered to determine that Turner was indeed an active accomplice in the piratical acts of William Kidd. He was sent to London to stand trial before the Court of Admiralty, where he was tried, declared guilty, and hanged.

When Kidd set his ship into the shallows of the Chesapeake, Turner had not been the only crew member to have departed with his share of the booty. Both Maryland and Virginia worried about reports that as many as sixty deserters and more than a few pirates who had been captured and subsequently escaped jail were intending to swarm into the Tidewater region. The possible presence of the infamous Captain Kidd and sixty deserters from his crew in the region had also become a concern for Robert Quary of the Vice Admiralty Court of Pennsylvania. With the aid of Governor Jeremiah Basse of New Jersey, he was able to capture four of the pirates at Cape May. He wrote:

And [I] might have with Ease secured all the rest of them, and the ship too, had not this Government given me the Least aide or assistance, but they [did] not, or soe much as Issue out a Proclamation. But on the Contrary the People of the Government have Entertain'd the Pyrates, Conveyed them from place to place, Furnish'd them with Provisions and Liquors given them Inteli'gence and sheltered them from Justice, and now the greatest part of them are conveyed away in Boats to Road Island [sic]. All the person[s] That I have affronted and call'd Enemies to the Country for Disturbing and hindring honest men (as They are pleased to call the Pyrates) from bringing their money and Settling amongst them.

Judging from Quary's words, it seems that the deserter pirates were able to purchase cooperation from local officials and citizens alike. Certainly the rumored individual shares of loot amounting to 4,000 pounds sterling per man would have financed a lot of bribes and purchased a tremendous welcome and goodwill.

In his hunt for the remaining pirates, Quary dispatched an express to Governor Nicholson of Virginia begging him to immediately send a man-of-war to patrol the Delaware River. Nicholson responded by sending the *Essex Prize* "to look About for Sixty Pyrates (which belonged to one Captain Kidd) who came from Madagascar." But by the time the *Essex Prize* got there the Delaware was empty and the pirates were gone.

Unbeknownst to colonial authorities, Kidd had sailed for Boston, stopping briefly en route at Gardiners Island off the coast of New York Colony. Although Kidd's friend and coinvestor, Governor Coote, the Earl of Bellomont, was in Boston, he was well aware of the accusations against Kidd and was justifiably afraid of being implicated in his associate's acts of piracy. Bellomont reasoned that his best chance of saving his own neck was to send Kidd to England in chains.

Kidd's sloop arrived in Boston on July 1, 1699, but Kidd did not go to the governor's house until the evening of July 3. The next day, he gave Bellomont a detailed narrative of the voyage and the names of his crew and the mutineers. Several days later, Bellomont issued an arrest warrant, and a shocked Captain Kidd was taken to jail and all his possessions were seized. The governor sent a letter informing the Board of Trade in England that he had captured the infamous William Kidd.

Kidd attempted to escape from jail and was moved to Stone Prison, where he was put in irons and denied all visitors. Kidd's wife, Sarah, petitioned for the return of the belongings she had brought to her husband's ship, which had been confiscated along with his other holdings. Although she had no communication with Kidd, Sarah seems to have remained steadfastly loyal to him while he languished in his unheated cell, waiting for a chance to clear his name. On February 16, 1700, he was taken aboard HMS *Advice*, on which he endured the long crossing to London while chained to the wall of a cabin. Sarah never got to say good-bye.

Kidd's return to England threatened to cause a political scandal because of his links to King William and the four powerful Whig politicians who had backed his voyage. In a deposition taken during a seven-hour grilling before the Lords of the Admiralty, Kidd said that he "was employed for the seizing of pirates . . . only as to his own committing piracy he would excuse himself that his seamen forced him to what was done." The Tories accused the Whigs of hiring a pirate to steal for them. Robert Harley, Speaker of the House of Commons, said, "Captain Kidd was commander under the Great

Seal of England to go against pirates at Madagascar. . . . That several great men were to have shares with him, amongst whom the pirates' goods were to be divided, whereas by law, they should [have been] returned to the owners. . . . It is said the Great Seal [Somers] and others are concerned in it." The true reasons for Kidd's arrest and imprisonment had become clear: He was a pawn in the political maneuverings of the British Parliament and, like all pawns, he was entirely expendable. Kidd was imprisoned in Newgate Prison and held in solitary confinement. He could write only to the Admiralty, and no one was permitted to talk with him.

While imprisoned, Kidd told authorities that a small portion of his fabulous treasure was hidden on Gardiners Island, New York, where a friend was safeguarding it. In fact, Kidd had left it in the care of John Gardiner, who owned the island. He cooperated with British authorities in retrieving the loot. In accordance with Kidd's instructions, gold and other treasure worth in excess of 10,000 pounds sterling was dug up on Gardiners Island and sent to England to pay off his investment backers in the hope of ensuring their loyalty. This seems to have had the opposite effect from what Kidd intended. Some of the backers refused to accept the payment, fearing it might implicate them in Kidd's actions. Those who did receive payment simply saw it as a just return on their investment and wanted nothing more to do with the matter. In total, 1,111 ounces of gold, 2,353 ounces of silver, one pound of assorted gemstones, fifty-seven bags of sugar, and forty-one bales of cloth were shipped to the English Treasury. Precisely how much of Kidd's Gardiners Island fortune may have remained on the island is unknown.

Kidd also indicated that further treasures were hidden in Virginia, New Jersey, Maryland, and elsewhere, and that they could be retrieved if only someone would step forward to intercede on his behalf, although this may have been a desperate political maneuver. But as with the Gardiners Island treasure, no one wanted to ally himself with Kidd even for the sake of a vast fortune, so knowledge of the exact location of the rest of Kidd's treasure remained his and his alone.

On March 27, 1701, one day short of a year after entering New-gate Prison, Kidd became history's only accused pirate to testify before Britain's House of Commons. The four hundred members of Parliament shouted questions, and although no precise transcript exists, we know that Kidd denied being a pirate and refused to implicate his backers in the supposed scandal in the hope that his show of loyalty to his investors would persuade them to intercede on his behalf. But like most political loyalties, it was naïve and wholly misplaced.

William Kidd's trial began on May 8 and ended the following day. Five prosecutors tried him, and nine others—six loyal members of his crew and three mutineers—testified. Kidd refused to plead until he had the French passes taken from the *Quedagh Merchant*, but eventually he pleaded not guilty. For two years, Kidd had been accused of being a pirate, but now the primary charge against him was not for piracy, but for the murder of gunner William Moore. The jury brought in a unanimous guilty verdict.

Kidd was then tried again, this time for piracy. Doctor Newton, the prosecutor, said Kidd had "committed many great piracies and robberies, taking the ships and goods of the Indians and others . . . and torturing cruelly their persons to discover if anything had escaped his hands; burning their houses, and killing after a bar-barous manner the Natives on shore; equally cruel, dreaded and hated both on land and at sea. These criminal attempts and actions have rendered his name . . . too well known [and] he is now looked upon as an Arch Pirate and Common Enemy of Mankind."

After this withering—and creatively enhanced—opening state-ment, Newton called his witnesses. Doctor Bradinham testified that Kidd had fired on English ships, kidnapped an English captain, tor-tured passengers, executed a native who had been tied to a tree, and burned a village. He denied any knowledge of the French passes, but Kidd's former crewman, Joseph Palmer, confirmed that Kidd had taken them. This second jury found Kidd guilty in thirty minutes.

Having been found guilty of two capital crimes, Kidd's prosecu-tors reportedly turned to him and inquired, "Thou hast been indicted for several Piracies and Robberies, and Murder, and hereupon hast been convicted. What hast thou to say for thyself, why shouldest thou not die according to law?"

Kidd replied, "I have nothing to say, but that I have been sworn against by perjured and wicked People."

The sentence, as expected, was death by hanging. Kidd's only comment on hearing his fate was "My Lord, it is a very hard sentence. For my part, I am the innocentest person of them all, only I have been sworn against by perjured persons."

During the trial, a member of Parliament had said of Kidd, "I thought him only a knave. I now know him to be a fool as well."

Kidd's execution was set for late afternoon on Friday, May 23. Having drunk a considerable amount of rum before and during the three-mile procession to Execution Dock, he slurred his words while giving his last speech, in which he blamed his mutinous crew for his troubles and named his New York patrons, Robert Livingston and the colony's governor general, the Earl of Bellomont, as villains. When Kidd had finished, the hangman yanked away the blocks holding up the platform, and Kidd and three others being executed with him dropped. Kidd's rope broke and he fell to the ground, but the reprieve was short lived. The executioner immediately picked him up, affixed another rope, and promptly hanged him again. His corpse was hung in an iron gibbet at Tilbury Point to serve as a deterrent—"as a greater Terrour to all Persons from Committing ye like Crimes for the time to come."

And so ended the short and rather ineffective career of the notorious Captain William Kidd. But Kidd's undignified end marked the beginning of his legend. For four centuries, people have wondered what became of the buried treasures he claimed to have secreted away along the American coast. The truth about Kidd's supposed treasure—both its size and its whereabouts—seems to have gone to the grave (or the gibbet) with Captain Kidd.

Richard Worley

Like any good businessman, Richard Worley started out small but paid close attention to business. He persevered, and, before long, became a notable success in his chosen field of endeavor—which happened to be piracy. In late September 1718 Worley and eight cohorts set out from New York in a small, open boat and made their way down the New Jersey coastline. They were ill equipped and carried almost no supplies. They survived by attacking and plundering local fishing boats, robbing them of their catches and provisions.

By the time Worley reached the Delaware Bay, he realized that his boat was too old and too small to be up to the job. Worley and his crew sailed up the Delaware River, where they captured a slightly better boat laden with someone's household goods. This small-time crime, like robbing fishing boats, did not classify as piracy because it did not take place in open waters and the boat was not a commercial trading vessel. Worley was still just a petty thief—but that was about to change.

Worley's next prize was far better suited to the needs of a would-be pirate with ambitions; it was a sloop sailing out of Philadelphia. With the taking of this newer, larger craft, Richard Worley graduated to the rank of pirate and added four additional men to his crew. Happy with his new, upwardly mobile lifestyle, Worley struck again only a few days later, taking a larger and better sloop, and he transferred his operations to the improved accommodations.

Worley's attacks may have been relatively small and insignificant, but his growing string of attacks nearly caused a panic when they were reported in Philadelphia. This was 1718 and the entire Atlantic seaboard was in a near-perpetual state of panic thanks to the dreaded Blackbeard; Worley's attacks, like almost every other seaborne crime of the day, was instantly attributed to that terror of the sea lanes. From Philadelphia word of these new pirate attacks spread to New York, and every time the news changed hands the perceived size of the menace grew. Determined to protect their livelihoods from this new danger, the merchants and ship owners of New York organized an expedition to hunt down and destroy the pirate vessel—be it Blackbeard's or someone else's—before it attacked their port or started picking off their ships at sea.

The pirate-hunting expedition that left the port of New York consisted of four small merchant vessels that had been refitted and were now heavily armed. For ten days the pirate-takers searched for their quarry, but they failed to sight any craft matching the description of Worley's ship. About the same time they returned to New York, Worley captured another sloop far to the south off the Virginia coast. Again he transferred his operations to his latest prize and, ironically, christened his new craft *New York's Revenge*.

Now in command of a really fine ship, "Captain" Worley decided that the most promising, and least protected, hunting ground lay in the busy merchant lanes of the Chesapeake Bay. Worley also cruised along both shores of the Delaware Bay and along the New Jersey coast, capturing any likely victim that was unlucky enough to cross his bow. For nearly three weeks Worley lived up to the dreaded image that had been built up around his first, modest attacks on the Delaware. Nothing was off limits. Attacking large and small craft both by day and by night, Worley and *New York's Revenge* disrupted waterborne traffic at will, molesting ships and their crews, taking anything of value, and selling the booty at a quick profit.

By now Worley's short history was being pieced together, and while it became obvious that this was not Blackbeard, the thought that one enterprising pirate could grow so quickly from a few men in a small, open launch to a major threat—which could well grow larger if Worley developed a whole fleet—sent a chill through coastal towns everywhere.

The newspapers in Philadelphia sensationalized the story of each new attack and capture, even though virtually no resistance had been offered by any of Worley's victims and almost all of the vessels had surrendered without a single shot being fired or any physical injury. In spite of the curious lack of violence, an outraged public demanded that authorities do something to bring a halt to this insufferable outrage. Considering that Worley had only been in operation for about three weeks, he had generated an amazing amount of publicity for himself. The governor of Pennsylvania was fully aware that the danger was not nearly as great as the public panic made it seem, but he was equally certain that he could not allow a pirate to roam free. Consequently a message was sent to the twenty-gun British warship HMS *Phoenix*, stationed at Sandy Hook, New Jersey, requesting that the Royal Navy move the ship down to the Delaware Bay and deal with the new pirate.

Obviously considering Worley to be a real and serious threat to lawful commerce, the Royal Navy complied with the request and moved the *Phoenix* south, along the New Jersey, Pennsylvania, and Maryland coasts, examining every cove, harbor, and inlet that might provide safe haven for a pirate ship. Perhaps Worley was aware that he was being hunted or perhaps he was just extremely lucky, but while the British were searching for his trail, the *New York's Revenge* was far out at sea, making its way south toward every pirate's favorite hunting grounds, the Bahamas.

In mid-November or early December 1718, Worley returned to America's Atlantic coast sailing his latest acquisitions, a new sloop and a brigantine, which he had taken in the Bahamas. To man these new craft Worley's crew had been expanded to twenty-five, and the new sloop boasted six cannon. A new sense of order had also been added. The crew had signed official pirate articles and the men were "on account" that they would fight to the death and that no quarter would be asked and none given.

Infused with this new, harder-edged sense of purpose, Worley returned toward the Chesapeake Bay with an eye to terrorizing the old, familiar shipping lanes and then fencing the stolen loot in the black markets of Philadelphia, Baltimore, and New York. But before returning to business as usual they would have to refit and resupply, so they docked at Charles Town (now Charleston), South Carolina.

When it came to dealing with pirates, Charles Town was not at all like the easily panicked New York and Philadelphia. Carolina governor Robert Johnson knew how to handle pirates. At the very time Worley pulled into Charles Town harbor the local prison was holding Blackbeard's former companion Stede Bonnet, who was awaiting trial. Fearing that Bonnet's impending trial—and certain execution—would prompt an attack by a force of pirates bent on freeing their comrade, Governor Johnson had written to the Royal Navy requesting the presence of a warship to guard Charles Town harbor. Before the Royal Navy could comply, a mid-level pirate named Moody had taken to prowling just beyond the mouth of the harbor, taking the occasional merchant vessel and making a nuisance of himself. The feeling in Charles Town was that Moody was waiting for the arrival of reinforcements and that together they would attack the city in an attempt to free Stede Bonnet.

With no time to wait for the arrival of the Royal Navy, and one known pirate in prison and another lurking outside the harbor, the governor and people of Charles Town decided to meet the threat on their own. Governor Johnson and the city council ordered a small fleet of ships to be outfitted as well as their budget would allow. Mimicking the pirate-hunting expedition that had been mounted in New York months earlier, four local merchant vessels were fitted with a total of sixty-eight cannon, provided with ammunition, and manned by volunteers. There were no experienced naval officers living or stationed in Charles Town, so experienced civilian merchant captains and officers would lead the crews. The ships chosen for the mission were the *King William*, the *Royal James*, the *Sea-Nymph* and the *Mediterranean*.

Even before Charles Town's fleet was ready to sail, Governor Johnson received the news that his preparations had not been made a moment too soon. Two unknown vessels, one a large ship and the other an armed sloop, had pulled into the outer harbor and were lying at anchor off Sullivan's Island. No one could identify the two craft but the general opinion was that either Moody had returned from a foraging expedition with new ships or some of his compatriots were starting to gather in preparation for a raid on the town and the prison. If the threat was to be dealt with, it would have to be done before more ships massed and Charles Town's four small pirate fighters would be outgunned and outmanned.

Anxious not to frighten the pirates away before they could be engaged in battle, the Charles Town fleet was disguised to look as much like its former merchant self as possible; the cannon were covered and most of the crew hid below decks. The *King William* was selected to lead the attack and Governor Johnson himself was on board the *Mediterranean*. As casually as possible, the four ships sailed out of the harbor and toward the pirates. When the two sides closed to within hailing distance Governor Johnson clearly heard the enemy demand their surrender. Johnson gave the signal to attack and instantly the situation changed. Covers were jerked off the cannon, heavily armed men poured out of the holds and onto the decks, the Union Jack ensign was hoisted from the masts, and sixty-eight cannon opened fire on two very surprised pirate ships.

The larger of the two pirate ships had run so close to her intended prey that two of Governor Johnson's ships, the *Sea-Nymph* and the *Royal James*, were able to maneuver between her and the open sea and cut off her avenue of retreat. Though the pirate ship found itself trapped, it certainly did not lack the will to fight. As fast as the Charles Town ships poured cannonballs and musket fire among the pirates, the pirates returned fire shot for shot. For four hours, the roar of cannon, the grinding crunch of shattering timbers, and the discharge of musketry continued, amid smoke so thick that that it was nearly impossible for the competing sides to see each other. Rolling with the impact of the cannon fire and unable to navigate, the ships came perilously close to colliding again and again while the anxious crowds gathered on the Charles Town docks and quaysides watched the battle with mounting excitement and fear.

Eventually, through careful seamanship and sheer bravery, the colonists managed to pair two of their ships against each of the pirate vessels. The *Royal James* and the *Sea-Nymph* positioned themselves so they could rake the deck of the larger pirate ship with round after round of musket and cannon shot. Faced with this continuous wall of withering fire, many of the pirates were forced to abandon the fight and take shelter below the deck of their shattered ship in an effort to save themselves. With the pirate ship's decks nearly abandoned, the *Royal James* and *Sea-Nymph* closed on the enemy and their crews swarmed over the gunwales and across the decks. The pirate captain and some of his fiercest men refused to surrender and stood fighting until they were cut down.

While the larger pirate ship was being taken, her smaller companion seemed to be faring better. Slipping out of the fray, she broke for open water, desperately trying to avoid the fate of her companion. But Governor Johnson had no intention of allowing the ship to escape long enough to warn other pirates or gather reinforcements. Ordering his own *Mediterranean* and the *King William* into full pursuit, he chased the fleeing pirates, matching their movements and slowly closing the distance between them. When the faster *King William* closed to within firing distance the pirates realized that escape was impossible. They hauled down the black flag and surrendered their vessel.

When Johnson and his men boarded the captured enemy they were amazed to find that this was not one of Moody's ships, but an English-registered prison transport that had only recently been captured on its way to deliver a load of convicts to the colonies. Many of the "pirates" turned out to be freed convicts who had willingly joined their captors; the ship's terrified crew and officers had been locked below decks.

Governor Johnson and his ships returned, with their prizes in tow, to a tumultuous greeting in Charles Town. Amazingly, there was still one more surprise waiting for Johnson and his townspeople on a day that had offered far more excitement than they had anticipated. This was the news that while the ships they had taken had not been Moody's, they had been those of the far more feared Captain Richard Worley, who had plagued northern waters and sent fear through the ports of five colonies. And so came to an end the short, brutal, and memorable career of Richard Worley.

Joseph Wheland Jr. and the Tory Picaroons

"We anchored in the Chesapeake, after a most favorable passage, and the next day proceeded up as high as Lynnhaven." Thus wrote British general Alexander Leslie of his arrival in bay waters with 2,500 soldiers and a strong Royal Navy task force on October 20, 1780. Leslie's orders were to destroy rebel munitions supplies at Richmond and Petersburg in Virginia and establish a permanent military post on the Elizabeth River to aid in Britain's battle against the rebellious colonists and their attempt to gain independence. For the so-called "picaroons" of the Tidewater area the presence of the British, especially the naval squadron commanded by Captain George Gayton, rekindled flickering loyalties to the Crown. Within days of Gayton's arrival, the lower and central bay region, particularly in Tory hotbeds along the Eastern Shore, literally swarmed with the predatory barges, galleys, and privateer boats of English sympathizers. Some began to probe as high as the Patuxent on the western shore, while others contented themselves with raids, plundering, and foraging into the heart of the defenseless Delmarva Peninsula.

For Maryland, the British return to the bay came at a most inopportune time, as the state's naval defenses had practically ceased to exist. Never very large, by early 1780 the state navy, with the exceptions of the little schooners *Dolphin* and *Platter*, had all been auctioned off. Virginia, against which the main thrust of the enemy was directed, could no longer defend the expanse of the lower bay. Now, the Chesapeake was subjected not only to assault by the powerful land and sea forces of the British, but also to the "numberless Depredations committed with Impunity by Picaroons." Everywhere else the marauders known as picaroons were just called pirates, but in the lower tidewater area of the Chesapeake Bay they somehow acquired the nickname picaroon, a corruption of the early seventeenth-century Spanish word *picaron*, meaning a roguish adventurer.

One of the first targets on the revitalized picaroons' map was the Patuxent River, one of Maryland's most important commercial waterways. Of its 110-mile length, nearly half was accessible to seagoing ships as large as 300 tons displacement, and it sliced directly through the very heart of the western shore's richest, most productive tobacco-growing regions. The little towns dotting its banks, such as St. Leonard, Benedict, Huntingtown, Nottingham, Upper and Lower Marlboro, Pig Point, and Queen Anne's, were among the most prosperous in the central tidewater region. Its waters were deep, its plantations numerous, and, best of all for the picaroons, it was practically defenseless.

On November 5, 1780, the picaroons entered the mouth of the Patuxent, probing only as high as Point Patience, a narrow finger of sand projecting into the river from the Calvert County peninsula. The raiders landed without warning, burned the home of local planter John Parran, and seized two vessels laden with eighty hogsheads of tobacco. Retreating downriver, they demanded provisions from Col. William Fitzhugh's estate, Rousby Hall. When Fitzhugh refused, they bombarded his house with cannon and burned what was left.

With the assistance of local Tory pilots from St. Mary's and Calvert Counties, the raiders prowled the mouths of the Patuxent and Potomac for weeks on end, pouncing on any unsuspecting prey that sailed their way. The ad hoc blockade was so effective that on January 3, 1781, Joseph Ford, Maryland Commissary of Purchases for St. Mary's County, complained to Annapolis that the "enemies Barges so closely watch Patuxent and Potomac Rivers, [that it] is too dangerous to send forward supplies."

Among those Tories who had taken heart from the resurgence of Royal Navy power on the bay was Joseph Wheland Jr., who had been freed after nearly five years of confinement for loyalist sympathies and acts of piracy thanks to a £10,000 bond posted on his behalf by Samuel Covington and Thomas Holbrook. Only a month earlier Wheland had appeared willing to renounce his loyalist leanings in a meeting with Colonel George Dashiell, of Somerset County, in which he tried to explain away his former actions. Wheland insisted he was never involved in any attacks on patriot shipping and was only on board the loyalist ship as a captive, locked in irons below decks. It had all been a terrible mistake. After his bond was posted, Wheland was released and his boat returned to him. To prove his supposed loyalty, Wheland moved his family up the Wicomico River, far from the dreaded picaroons, and told Dashiell he would gladly fight against the Tories and contribute to the expense of building a barge to be used against them.

George Dashiell was completely taken in by Wheland's flimsy story, and sent a letter to Maryland governor Lee exonerating the crafty picaroon. Only days after commending Wheland to the governor, Dashiell received an urgent letter from Colonel Henry Hooper, the commander of Dorchester County, ordering him to arrest Wheland. Enclosed with the letter was an affidavit from a Captain Valentine Peyton of Stafford County, Virginia, who had been captured by Wheland on August 31 off Poplar Island. Soon afterward, a ship owned by Captain Oakley Haddaway had been seized by Wheland, as well as one belonging to Mr. William Barnes. It seemed Joe Wheland had returned to his nefarious activities without a second thought and was now in command of a pilot boat fitted with a jib sail and manned by a small crew of veteran Tories.

Emboldened by Wheland's success, others of his kind followed suit. Among these was John Botsworth, a onetime ship's carpenter from Annapolis who had piloted British raiders up the Annemessex. Once, when a vessel Botsworth was piloting had gone into action against an American vessel, he had himself placed in chains so that in the event of capture he could claim he had been pressed into service; he may very well have learned the trick from Wheland.

Wheland was soon working frequently in close concert with heavily armed barges of British sympathizers. To keep their identity secret they arranged signals of recognition, such as hoisting and lowering the mainsail three times in quick succession, that could be used as the occasion demanded. With a growing string of successful raids, Wheland became the undisputed king of the picaroons and gathered a loyal following and a small but deadly flotilla of four barges. In addition to the barge Wheland commanded, the other three each were led by one of his trusted lieutenants, Shadrack Horseman or the brothers Michael and William Timmons.

Wheland's activities had caused damage and physical injury to friend and foe alike, even before he turned to outright piracy. On December 11, Samuel Covington and Thomas Holbrook were obliged to acknowledge themselves to be indebted to the State of Maryland for £5,000 each if the picaroon captain did not appear before Governor Lee and his council "to answer a charge of high treason." Wheland, of course, failed to appear, and the bond was presumably forfeited.

By the end of 1780 there seemed to be no sanctuary for patriot shipping anywhere on the Chesapeake. The *Pennsylvania Gazette* reported: "Several of the enemy's small armed vessels have recently visited Oxford and other places on the Eastern Shore, Poplar Island in the Chesapeake and the Mouth of the Patuxent, on the Western Shore of this State, at all of which places their crews committed the greatest outrages. Not content with plundering the inhabitants of their Negroes, cattle and other property, they savagely laid several of their inhabitants in ashes."

On January 11, 1781, the Maryland Council learned that the notorious traitor Benedict Arnold had taken command of an army said to be nearly three thousand strong. He had already taken Richmond and sent a sizable force to capture Petersburg. Virginia was in a state of panic and towns along the Rappahannock and Potomac

Rivers, such as Fredericksburg and Alexandria, feared imminent attack. Maryland warned its county commanders that an invasion of the state was expected. Relay systems were set up along the Potomac to warn of the enemy's approach. And the enemy did approach.

On January 22, a British frigate drove three Maryland vessels aground at Cedar Point, near the mouth of the Patuxent, and destroyed two of them. Raids were carried out on plantations at Point Lookout and Smith Creek, on the Potomac. A schooner was seized and burned several days later on the St. Mary's River and more raids were carried out in St. Mary's County.

The plundering and hit-and-run attacks continued unabated on the eastern and western shores of the Chesapeake Bay, and Joseph Wheland seemed to be constantly in the thick of the action. Colonel Joseph Dashiell (not to be confused with Colonel George Dashiell) was infuriated by Wheland's inauspicious reappearance. On March 4, Dashiell wrote to Governor Lee at Cedar Point, near the mouth of the Patuxent:

> Joseph Wheland that old offender is down in Somerset plundering again and we have reason to believe that the Gaoler in Baltimore is alone to blame as Wheland's Father informed one of our Neighbours that he let him go at large sum time before he Came away if this practice is followed no one will venture to take any of them up and send them forward as they will be there to suffer for it. If I had Directions to go into Somerset, I think I could apprehend him, as he has lately robed a certain Thomas Reuker who I think would assist me to Trap him.

Dashiell was equally distraught over a nest of Tories who had taken up residence on the islands in Tangier Sound. Citing the recent robbery of local citizen Plannor Williams by a band of nine picaroons from the sound, he told the governor, "whenever your Excellency & Council propose to Remove the people and stock of the Islands I should be Glad to assist with all my heart as I consider them at this time the most Dangerous Enemy we have to watch the Motions off—and am Certain if they Can do us no other Damage they will rob & Plunder all they Can before they are removed."

Neighboring Somerset County was being constantly savaged by hit-and-run raids, for which Dashiell repeatedly blamed British privateers and picaroons from the larger islands in the sound. The events of Saturday morning, March 10, 1781,when a joint privateer-picaroon expedition assaulted the town of Vienna, would prove he was right on both counts.

The invaders approached the town by water, coming up the Nanticoke in a brig and two sloops, one of them newly built and armed with fourteen 18-pounders. They opened the attack with a heavy bombardment of the town, using both round and grapeshot. A few resolute militiamen, commanded by Colonel John Dickinson and Captain William Smoot, gathered along the riverbank in an attempt to repel the invaders. When an enemy barge loaded with men rowed toward the shore, the defenders opened fire. Three times the enemy attempted to land, and three times they were beaten back. Finally, the intense fire from the ships drove the defenders back, and the barge reached the shore.

Three of the attackers were wounded and one was killed, and the defenders suffered one death. Colonel Henry Hooper, who apparently arrived on the scene just before the landing, learned that another privateer brig was guarding the mouth of the river, preventing possible relief or rescue by water. When the enemy pulled onto the shore the exhausted militiamen waved a flag of truce. The picaroons said they wanted nothing more than the grain stored in the town. If the militiamen would give it up, the invaders would leave part of it for the inhabitants and leave Vienna in peace. They even promised to pay the market price for the grain, but insisted that if the defenders refused to deal the town would be burned to the ground and everything in it destroyed. Hooper realized his force "could defend nothing, the Town and Grain lying under the command of their Vessels we agreed to their Terms."

The raiders carried off between 900 and 1,000 bushels of Indian corn while the humiliated militiamen stood watching helplessly. The invaders expressed disappointment that there had not been more grain stored in the town and they hinted broadly that they might try the Choptank or Wicomico rivers for additional grain supplies. True to their word, on Monday morning the invaders departed, leaving Vienna intact.

Joseph Dashiell, who was frantically resisting landings from the raiders all along the shores of Worcester County, was infuriated by the surrender of Vienna and blamed Hooper for the militia's retreat: "The Lieutenant of that County arrived and ordered the Militia to retreat as I am told, & has made a Capitulation that in my Opinion will Disgrace us, & be attended with the worst Consequences."

With each success the British and their loyalist allies grew bolder. As the Maryland state government rushed to mobilize more and better defenses the port of Annapolis was being blockaded by enemy warships. The Elk River area was threatened and landings were being carried out on Poole's Island and in Harford County. Scenes of chaos and disorder were repeated throughout the central and upper bay region—a schooner run ashore by Tory barges here, a refugee with all his belongings forced to flee before the marauders there, and everywhere towns were looted, homes burned, and waterborne commerce throttled by picaroons, privateers, and the Royal Navy.

By early April, Maryland's two principal waterways, the Potomac and Patuxent, were being simultaneously brutalized. On Saturday, April 7, a picaroon barge, manned principally by blacks but commanded by Captain Jonathan Robinson, a white man, probed far up the Patuxent, wreaking havoc among the local population. When the alarm sounded, riverfront homes from Swanson's Creek northward to Upper Marlboro were abandoned amid scenes of wild panic. As far up as Lower Marlboro, the picaroons landed unopposed and plundered towns and homesteads. The home of Captain John David, former commander of the Maryland galley *Conqueror,* was burned to the ground, along with an unsuspecting traveler sleeping inside. Colonel Peregrine Fitzhugh and William Allein, a local merchant, were taken prisoner (though they were later released). All of the vessels docked at Lower Marlboro, including one fully laden with provisions, were captured and tobacco in the local warehouse was stolen. On Sunday morning the exhausted raiders set off down the river with a strong northwest wind behind them and their holds crammed with tons of goods and a band of slaves that had belonged to Colonel Fitzhugh.

"Every hours experience," wrote Stephen West, a leader and civic bulwark of the Patuxent mercantile community, "shows the necessity of having some Armed Vessels in the great Rivers especially the Patuxent and Potowmack." His assessment was correct; the picaroon barge escaped unscathed and on the following day rendezvoused with two ships and a brig at the river's mouth. That evening, the barge landed a few miles to the south at Cedar Point and its occupants burned the home of Nicholas Sewell.

Nearly identical attacks were carried out by Tory privateers prowling the Potomac. Raids were carried out as far upriver as Alexandria, followed by a series of landings at various places along both shores of the river. Homes and plantations were plundered and burned, slaves stolen, and civilians carried off as prisoners. At Young's Ferry, Hooe's Ferry, Robert Washington's plantation, and Port Tobacco, the picaroons swarmed ashore and any organized opposition gave way under their repeated attacks.

Finally, in the latter part of April, the raiders withdrew, the holds of their ships and barges filled with plunder. It had been a miserable experience for Maryland and Virginia, both of which had been entirely unprepared to meet the emergency. "I expect we shall have frequent visits from these plundering Banditts," wrote Thomas Stone of Maryland after the raiders' departure. "I hope we will so well prepare as to repel their attacks that they will find the business as unprofitable as it is disgraceful."

It was a vain hope. Despite the best intentions of the nearly impotent Maryland government to blunt the assault of the picaroons and privateers, it was becoming painfully evident that the burden of naval defense would have to fall on the local inhabitants. The Eastern Shore, isolated from the state government and frequently cut off from outside help, was particularly vulnerable. "Local circumstances render it Difficult," wrote Dorchester County leaders Robert Goldsborough and Gustavus Scott, "for the Inhabitants of this Shore, exposed as they are to the utmost Calamities of War & Piracies to expect assistance from our more powerfull neighbours of the western shore." Dorchester County, with 1,700 effective fighting men (of which only 150 were armed), reflected the deadly vulnerability to attack of all the Eastern Shore counties without naval protection.

One of the first major efforts to address regional defenses took place in Somerset County. On March 21, 1781, twenty-six of the county's leading citizens, stirred to action by the mounting attacks against their region by picaroons and privateers, proposed to the Maryland Council a scheme fathered by Captain Zedekiah Walley. Walley's plan was to build a fifty-foot barge capable of carrying sixty men and a twenty-four-pound bow gun to protect county waters. Whalley calculated that the vessel could be built for less than £150 and volunteered to oversee the construction himself. Though the state was sympathetic to the proposal, there was no money in the treasury. Consequently the people of Somerset undertook the project on their own.

The barge, built at Snow Hill, was dubbed *Protector* and she was destined to sail with distinction and success. On one occasion the *Protector* drove the picaroon raiders out of the Pocomoke region and captured several prizes. Taking heart from Somerset's self-reliance, Queen Anne's and Talbot Counties joined forces to purchase and maintain a barge called *Experiment* and build a number of boats for their own protection. These vessels were stationed in Eastern Bay and cruised between Kent Point and Tilghman Island. Dorchester County followed suit, with the construction of the barge *Defence.* Eventually, more barges, either captured from the enemy or, later, constructed with the help of state funds, began to appear in bay waters, vessels with names like *Intrepid, Terrible,* and *Fearnaught.*

It had been apparent, even before the Lower Marlboro raid, that the western shore of the Patuxent River needed a standing defense system to counter picaroon incursions. The first areas to consider taking matters into their own hands were Prince George's and

Calvert Counties. Like their counterparts on the Eastern Shore, twenty-three desperate merchants and gentlemen convened a meeting at the river port of Nottingham on April 21. Calling themselves the Board of Patuxent Associators and led by Colonel William Fitzhugh, the group secured permission from the Governor of Maryland to manage their own regional defenses, impress vessels, move equipment, and protect the Patuxent.

While the Board of Patuxent Associators worked to improve the river's defenses against the picaroons, the battle raged on. On April 25, off the mouth of the river, two American privateer schooners, the *Antelope* and the *Felicity*, challenged a loyalist New York privateer called *Jack-a-Lanthorn* carrying six guns and thirty-six men, along with a small prize sloop. The two American privateers had already captured a British ship called *Resolution* in the lower bay, and when they encountered and took the New Yorker, they not only relieved the Patuxent region of a potential attacker, but enriched their owners through the sale of the new prizes.

The Board of Patuxent Associators were constantly frustrated by a lack of funds, state support, and armament, supplies, and vessels. But the members pressed ahead. Artillery was mounted at strategic positions on the river. Beacons were erected at appropriate locations to provide early warning of intruders. And plans were made to locate a forty-foot armed barge and a whaleboat to serve as lookouts. A committee was sent to Baltimore to examine the recently captured *Jack-a-Lanthorn* for possible purchase, but the price was too high. On May 10, the board's agents, Samuel Maynard and Renaldo Johnson, purchased a ship, a battered schooner called *Nautilus*, salvaged from the shoals of Cedar Point, where she had been run aground by a British warship in January. This vessel, with a displacement of eighty-five tons, was armed with eight 3-pounders. The price was right, and an agreement was struck with her owners, Dorsey Wheeler and Company and Thomas Worthington. The ship was exchanged for 357,000 pounds of tobacco.

Captain John David of Lower Marlboro was hired to command the vessel and pilot her down the picaroon-infested bay to the Patuxent. But apparently no one bothered to consult with Captain David before assigning him the task, for he had already engaged to serve in another vessel. By the end of May, *Nautilus* was still lying at Fells Point, Baltimore. A barge and a whaleboat had yet to be procured. When *Nautilus* finally reached the Patuxent, her suitability as a guard ship was apparently questionable, for on August 11 she was put up for sale at Nottingham by the board. With the sale of *Nautilus*, the intended fulcrum of the Patuxent naval defense, the efforts of the short-lived Board of Associators to protect their river collapsed.

The fear of an invasion of Maryland lingered throughout the early summer of 1781. County militia units were held in readiness to march at a moment's notice, and commissaries were directed to purchase or seize all supplies in the event of attack to prevent them from falling into enemy hands. British warships again appeared on the Potomac in early June, dispatching armed barges to conduct foraging raids or simply to plunder and terrorize the civilian population. Within weeks the British disappeared, but the picaroons, hovering like birds of prey, swooped in to pick up the leavings.

In July, the notorious Joseph Wheland struck again. This time the victim was *Greyhound*, "a beautiful boat laden with Salt, Peas, Pork, Bacon and some Dry Goods." Captured in Hooper's Strait, the skipper and his crew were detained for twenty-four hours aboard Wheland's barge, during which time one of the passengers, a Mr. Furnival, was robbed of his money and watch, "and indeed every Thing that the Thieves could lay their Hands on." The captain of the schooner and his men were set ashore at Dames Quarter. Furnival later reported that while being held captive he "saw several other Bay craft fall into the Fangs of the same Vultures."

As the picaroon attacks continued, pressure increased for the Maryland government to act. The region between the mouth of the Patuxent south to Tangier Sound had become a virtual no-man's-land through which shipping passed at its own risk. In early July, Samuel Smith of Baltimore informed Governor Lee that two of his ships, carrying cargos of tobacco, had been taken. "This is a heavy loss to my business," he complained. "They were taken just coming out of Patuxent by three Barges full of Men one of which went down & the other two up to burn Capt. [Jeremiah] Yellet's Brig."

Typical of the reports passing daily through the Maryland chief executive's office was one from Colonel Joseph Dashiell which informed Governor Lee that "there is four privatars and as many Barges in our sound [and] they have plundered the Houses of Leven Gale & Levin Dashiell & Burned all the Houses of the Latter yesterday morning." Not only were picaroons becoming bolder, but the barbarity of their actions seemed to be increasing as well. In mid-July Captain Gale of the Somerset County Militia was physically dragged from his bed by a protégé of Joseph Wheland, one Captain John McMullen, commander of the picaroon barge *Restoration*, accompanied by thirteen crewmen. The unfortunate militiaman was hauled off to Clay Island, "where he was most inhumanly whipt six lashes" and then hanged until they believed him dead. Soon after he was cut down, he revived. McMullen attempted to persuade his crew to hang their victim again, but they refused. He proposed drowning the poor man, but again they refused. Finally, Gale was released after taking an oath not to bear arms against the King.

Wheland, McMullen, and Robinson frequently acted in concert now, rendezvousing at Courtney's Island before setting out on a joint cruise. Wheland and his chief lieutenant, William Timmons Jr., occasionally preferred the mobility of a small whaleboat to the larger barge, and visited carefully selected sites along the Eastern Shore, defended or not, with relative impunity. They did not discriminate in the selection of their men, and frequently employed black slaves whom they had freed during their attacks as crewmen. Indeed, the black picaroons proved to be so ferocious in battle that they terrified their white opponents, a trait that made them particularly valuable to Wheland. Neither were the picaroons particular in their selection of victims. Eventually, for Joseph Wheland, it wouldn't even matter whether his prey was patriot or Tory.

At long last the State of Maryland fielded its first official barges since it sold off its navy in 1778 and 1779. The flotilla's first expedition, initiated on July 28, 1781, was designed specifically to rid the bay of the picaroons. Commodore George Grason of the Maryland Navy was given command. The flotilla was to be composed of the barges *Intrepid* and *Terrible*, and Grason's own flagship *Revenge*. Two days after sailing, on July 30, the little squadron engaged two pica-roon barges, a whaleboat, and two smaller vessels. By chance they had fallen in with the bay area's most notorious pirates, Joseph Wheland, Robinson, and John McMullen. The barge *Restoration*, captained by McMullen, and two other, smaller boats were taken. Robinson, who was in the second barge, and Wheland, who was in the whaleboat, escaped during the fight. Euphoria over this victory was contagious on the Eastern Shore. "The event has given general joy," wrote Matthew Tilghman on August 3, "and if we cannot flat-ter ourselves with peace, we begin to think we have a chance of remaining safe from the plunderers that have late infested us."

But the picaroons were not intimidated by a single defeat and did not slow their attacks. In late August they returned to the Patuxent River, leaving the area only after capturing three vessels laden with tobacco. On August 27, two barges pushed up the Nanticoke to Vienna, plundered the town, and captured two or three fully laden vessels lying in the river there. One of the barges proceeded up beyond the town and captured two more vessels, even as her sister barge retired downriver with her prizes. Belatedly alerted, Colonel Henry Hooper frantically collected a party of militiamen and retook three of the vessels. Then, posting troops on each side of the river, he effectively cut off the retreat of one of the barges, forcing the enemy to run her ashore and make their escape on foot. Three picaroons were captured and sent to Annapolis on August 31. After securing the barge, Hooper dispatched a party of light horse down the river, but the second barge and her prizes had disappeared.

At one o'clock the following morning, Hooper was awakened by a messenger with the news that the barge had returned in the night and taken the people of Vienna prisoner. The militia was ordered to reassemble and march to the town, but it was too late; the elusive picaroons had escaped again.

Farther south on the Chesapeake, Tory and privateer raids were conducted with a frequency and brutality increasingly motivated by a desire for plunder rather than devotion to the King and England. More and more the picaroon raids were being carried out against both sides. By the late summer of 1781 Gwynn's Island at the mouth of the Piankatank River was being used as a picaroon base for barge operations, which were increasingly directed against fellow Tories as well as patriots.

Many of the picaroons had degenerated from seaborne guerrillas to nothing more than pirates, plundering everyone and everywhere they pleased. In mid-June, General George Weedon of Virginia wrote that some "of their vessels are continually in the mouth of the river and I am convinced from many circumstances hold a correspondence with . . . inhabitants of Gwyn's Island and Middlesex." The loyalists of the region, as far away as Urbanna on the Rappahannock, a place patriots called a "sink" of Tory disaffection, were rapidly becoming disenchanted with their so-called allies at sea. On June 19, it was reported that numerous influential loyalists such as Ralph Wormley, John Randolph Grymes, Beverly Robinson, and the inhabitants of Urbanna had all been plundered by Tory picaroons. When Wormley and Robinson assembled a band of loyalists at Robinson's estate, "to consult a plan of recovery," the picaroons struck again "and plundered them a second time, without landing at any other house."

The reign of terror brought on by the pirate picaroons and privateers now disgusted the leaders of both sides. Even Lord Cornwallis, who had recently arrived at Portsmouth, Virginia, was shocked by their vindictive activities and commented in a letter to Sir Henry Clinton, British Commander in Chief in North America, that the "horrid enormity of our privateers in the Chesapeake Bay" was quite "prejudicial to his Majesty's service." Indeed, it was driving some loyalists away from the Crown and hardening the resolve of the American cause.

Cornwallis, however, had more important matters to occupy his time than the dirty little guerrilla war on the bay. He had an army to move, and a town to fortify—a little place on the York River called Yorktown.

Privateers of the Baltimore Hero

The Maryland privateering sloop *Baltimore Hero* was commissioned on September 16, 1776—only two months after the signing of the Declaration of Independence—and placed under the direction of Commander Thomas Waters of Baltimore. There was already no doubt that the struggle for independence would spill over the land and into the deep waters of the Atlantic, so *Baltimore Hero* was designed to be a prize-taking privateer and the official description of the ship makes her mission seem more than clear. The *Baltimore Hero* was listed as having a battery of six 3-pounder cannon and six swivel guns, and a crew of twenty men. For a small craft with a limited crew the *Hero* was very well armed. Serving as first mate was William Jones, John Pine was second mate, and John Sharp was third mate; all three of the men were from their ship's native city of Baltimore. The ship's 5,000-pound-sterling bond was executed by Commander Waters, Robert T. Hooe of Alexandria, Virginia, and John Crockett and Thomas Ringgold, both of Baltimore. On the same day the bond was recorded, Commander Waters received permission from the Maryland Council of Safety to sail for Martinique, in the French West Indies, or some other foreign port, apparently of his own choosing. Accordingly, the newly commissioned *Baltimore Hero* sailed down to the West Indies, calling at the neutral port of St. Eustatius in the Dutch West Indies, where she was refitted and resupplied before running out of the port to seize whatever prizes she could find and, hopefully, harass and infuriate the British.

On November 21, 1776, the *Hero* captured the English-registered brig (or brigantine) *May*, captained by William Taylor, about three miles from Sandy Point on the island of St. Christopher's in the British West Indies. Other accounts say the capture was in Dutch territorial waters and carried out right under the guns of the Dutch fort at St. Eustatius. Since Britain and Holland were allies, if this second account is true it would have been a shocking breach of protocol, but relations between the two European nations were already strained, and during wartime anything is possible. Wherever the *Baltimore Hero*'s attack on the *May* took place, the capture was seen from St. Christopher's and witnessed from St. Eustatius by that island's governor, Johannes de Graaff. The *Baltimore Hero*'s first prize was owned by Bendal and Foster McConnell of Dominica in the British West Indies, William Brown of Cork, Ireland, and Benson & Postlewait of Liverpool, England. When it was taken, the *May* had been en route from Dominica to St. Eustatius. Perhaps sensing the magnitude of the trouble this capture was likely to cause, Captain Waters seems to have identified himself to his English prisoners as Ezekiel John Dorsey, but there was no doubting the ship's allegiance. The *May* was brought back into St. Eustatius with the *Baltimore Hero* flying the American colors.

The *Baltimore Hero* was resting at St. Eustatius on December 1, 1776, and members of her crew were ashore, enjoying the local nightlife and bragging about their capture of the so-called "Irish brig" just offshore. This outrageous action brought a strong protest from Vice Admiral James Young, commander of the Royal Navy's Leeward Islands Station. On December 17, 1776, Governor Craister Greathead of St. Christopher's lodged another strong protest with Governor Johannes de Graaff of St. Eustatius. On December 19, Governor de Graaff ordered a full investigation into Captain Waters's activities, which, because it was a very poorly conceived a cover-up, brought some embarrassment to the Dutch.

Eventually the entire nasty affair blew over, Captain Waters escaped punishment, and the *Baltimore Hero* moved on. She was at St. Lucia about March 10, 1777, where it was reported as having eight guns and fifty men—so it seems to have picked up two cannon and thirty extra crewmen. Another report, dated April 9, 1777, puts her at Martinique, and gives her the same count of both guns and men. Yet another report, dated at London on May 24, 1777, indicates that a privateer named the *Baltimore*, with sixteen guns, had put into Bordeaux, France, in a "very leaky" condition—but it seems unlikely that this was the *Baltimore Hero* because of the excessive number of cannon.

On September 3, 1777, the British ship *Catherine*, captained by John Freeman, arrived from Tobago at British-occupied New York laden with a cargo of rum and sugar. Freeman reported that he had been captured on August 13 by a privateer sloop called the *Baltimore Hero*, commanded by "one Halsey." A lieutenant, a prize master, and three hands from the *Baltimore Hero* went aboard the *Catherine* as the prize crew but on August 22 the British crew overpowered their captors, recaptured the *Catherine*, and brought her safely into New York.

But such a small setback as the loss of a single prize could not stop the *Baltimore Hero*, which was recommissioned on May 15, 1779, and placed under the command of John Earle from Philadelphia. She was now said to weigh in at 80 tons displacement, she was rerigged to change her from a sloop to a schooner, her ever-increasing battery was now listed as fourteen guns, six swivels, and two cohorns, and she now had a crew of thirty men. William Britton of Philadelphia served as first mate. Her new owners were given as Benjamin and John Crockett, John Sterett, and others of Baltimore. The new 5,000-pound-sterling bond was posted by Earle and John Crockett.

On June 13, the new and improved *Baltimore Hero* put to sea on her way to St. Eustatius alongside a Maryland privateer brig named *Lively* under the command of James Belt. Accompanying the *Baltimore Hero* and the *Lively* was another Maryland privateer brig named *Lady Washington*, sailing under Commander Joseph Greenway. With the three privateers were four pilot boats. In the Chesapeake Bay, not far off the mouth of the Rappahannock River, the American privateers collided with two British privateers carrying twelve guns each. Sailing with the British were two American prize ships they had taken. The *Baltimore Hero* and the *Lively* swung into action and were apparently in the process of capturing the British privateers, when four more British vessels, two brigs and two schooners, intervened. The *Baltimore Hero* managed to recapture one of the British prizes, sending it into the Rappahannock River. The rest of the Americans retreated and the British chased them up to Point-No-Point before breaking off the engagement after more than two fruitless hours. The *Baltimore Hero* had three men wounded and had taken damage to her hull, rigging, and sails. The *Lively* had two men mortally wounded.

The Americans retreated to Annapolis and began refitting. The plan was to sail in a few days with additional privateers in their company. *Baltimore Hero* eventually made her voyage to St. Eustatius. In late October 1779, it was reported that *Baltimore Hero* arrived safely back at her home port of Baltimore.

George Little:
Yankee Privateer

Frequently an author's ability to accurately describe historical figures and events is limited by the scant amount of reliable information available beyond the most basic facts and figures. We are left with a sense of what and who and where but rarely a deep understanding of why things took the course that they did. Worse still, the historical figures we encounter often appear as caricatures or cartoons rather than actual people, and this is especially true when it comes to pirates and privateers. For this chapter, rather than simply recounting the story of American privateer George Little, we are fortunate enough to have found an excerpt from Little's own writings. Not only do we have a striking first-hand account of life on board several privateer ships but we get a glimpse of the skill required to man a sailing ship and just how little chance a privateer had of getting rich. Here then is a small taste of Little's life under the American ensign in the War of 1812, as excerpted from his autobiography, *Life on the ocean, or Twenty years at sea: being the personal adventures of the author.*

The story begins in late April or early May of 1812, about six or eight weeks before the U.S. declared war on Great Britain. Little was in South America, having just completed a voyage, when he received news that the Rio de Janeiro-based company employing him was bankrupt. The captain had his ship, cargo, and some of his personal belongings seized by creditors. Left with five hundred dollars to his name, Little booked passage back to the United States.

With this small sum I took passage in the ship Scioto, bound for Baltimore. I was induced to do this because little doubt was then entertained that there would be a war between the United States and England, and I was anxious to get home, if possible, before it was declared. We were fortunate enough to arrive in safety, although the war had been actually declared fifteen days before we got inside of the Capes of Virginia.

When we arrived in Baltimore, I found the most active preparations were in progress to prosecute the war. A number of privateers were fitting out; and every where the American flag might be seen flying, denoting the places of rendezvous; in a word, the most intense excitement prevailed throughout the city, and the position of a man was not at all enviable, if it were ascertained that he was in any degree favorably disposed towards the British. It happened to fall to my lot to be an eye-witness to the unpleasant affair of tarring and feathering a certain Mr. T. [John Thomson, tarred and feathered by a mob on July 28, 1812], and also to the demolishing of the Federal Republican printing office by the mob [on June 22].

Once more I returned to Boston, to see my friends, whom I found pretty much in the same situation as when I left them. Every persuasion was now used to induce me to change my vocation, backed by the strong reasoning that the war would destroy commerce, and that no alternative would be left for seamen but the unhallowed pursuit of privateering. These arguments had great weight, and I began to think seriously of entering into some business on shore; but then most insuperable difficulties arose in my mind as to the nature of the business I should pursue.

Unable to conceive of profitable employment on land, George Little returned to Norfolk, Virginia, in search of a commission on a privateering vessel. Little supported the American cause. The coming war seemed certain to be a conflict fought at sea. The British Royal

Navy constituted the single greatest military power in the world at the time, and without an equally strong navy of its own, the newly formed United States would face serious difficulties in the conflict. Little, an experienced seaman, did not have much trouble procuring an officer's position aboard a privateering ship.

Here too, in Norfolk, all was bustle and excitement—drums beating, colors flying, soldiers enlisting, men shipping in the States' service, and many privateers fitting out—creating such a scene of confusion as I had never before witnessed. Young, and of an ardent temperament, I could not look upon all these stirring movements an unmoved spectator; accordingly, I entered on board the George Washington privateer, in the capacity of first lieutenant. She mounted one twelve-pounder on a pivot, and two long nines, with a complement of eighty men.

She was in all respects a beautiful schooner, of the most exact symmetrical proportions, about one hundred and twenty tons' burden, and said to be as swift as any thing that floated the ocean. In reference to this enterprise, I must confess, in my cooler moments, that I had some qualms: to be sure, here was an opportunity of making a fortune; but then it was counterbalanced by the possibility of getting my head knocked off, or a chance of being thrown into prison for two or three years: however, I had gone too far to recede, and I determined to make the best of it. Accordingly, I placed what little funds I had in the hands of Mr. G., of Norfolk, and repaired on board of the privateer, with my dunnage contained in a small trunk and clothes-bag. On the morning of July 20th, 1812, the officers and crew being all on board, weighed anchor, made sail, and stood down the river, with the stars and stripes floating in the breeze, and was saluted with a tremendous cheering from the shore. I now was on board of a description of craft with which I was entirely unacquainted; I had, therefore, much to learn. The lieutenants and prize-masters, however, were a set of clever fellows; but the captain was a rough, uncouth sort of a chap, and appeared to me to be fit for little else than fighting and plunder.

The crew was a motley set indeed, composed of all nations; they appeared to have been scraped together from the lowest dens of wretchedness and vice, and only wanted a leader to induce them to any acts of daring and desperation. Our destination, in the first place, was to cruise on the Spanish main, to intercept the English traders between the West India Islands and the ports on the main. This cruising ground was chosen because, in case of need, we might run into Carthagena [on the northwest coast of present-day Colombia] to refit and water. When we had run down as far as Lynnhaven Bay [in southern Virginia], information was received from a pilot-boat that the British frigate Belvidere was cruising off the Capes. This induced our captain to put to sea with the wind from the southward, as the privateer's best sailing was on a wind.

On the morning of 22d of July, got under way from Lynnhaven Bay, and stood to sea. At 9 A.M., when about 10 miles outside of Cape Henry lighthouse, a sail was discovered directly in the wind's eye of us, bearing down under a press of canvass. Soon ascertaining she was a frigate, supposed to be the Belvidere, we stood on upon a wind until she came within short gunshot. Our foresail was now brailed up, and the topsail lowered on the cap; at the same time, the frigate took in all her light sails, and hauled up her courses.

As the privateer lay nearer the wind than the frigate, the latter soon dropped in our wake, and when within half-gunshot, we being under cover of her guns, she furled her topgallant sails; at the same moment we hauled aft the foresheet, hoisted away the topsail, and tacked. By this manoeuvre the frigate was under our lee. We took her fire, and continued to make short boards, and in one hour were out of the reach of her guns, without receiving any damage. This was our first adventure, and we hailed it as a good omen. The crew were all in high spirits, because the frigate was considered to be as fast as any thing on our coast at that time, and, furthermore, the captain had not only gained the confidence of the crew by this daring manoeuvre, but we found we could rely upon our heels for safety.

The privateer *George Washington* sailed south to the Mona Passage. There she came upon a sloop, nearly crashing into it in a heavy fog. Both ships rapidly exchanged a few shots to no effect before coming to the realization that they were both American vessels. The sloop, named the *Black Joke* and sailing out of New York, was also a privateer. The two ships agreed to cruise together in escort in the hopes of tracking down British trading vessels, but the *Black Joke* had difficulty keeping up with the swift-sailing *George Washington*. So they agreed to separate once again and to rendezvous at Cartegena.

In two days after parting with her, the long-wished-for cry of "Sail ho!" was sung out from the mast-head. Made all sail in chase. When within short gunshot, let her have our midship gun, when she immediately rounded to, took in sail, hoisted English colors, and seemed to be preparing to make a gallant defense.

In this we were not mistaken, for as we ranged up, she opened a brisk cannonading upon us. I now witnessed the daring intrepidity of Captain S.; for, while the brig was pouring a destructive fire into us, with the greatest coolness he observed to the crew, "That vessel, my lads, must be ours in ten minutes after I run this craft under her lee quarter." By this time we had sheered up under her stern, and received the fire of her stern-chasers, which did us no other damage than cutting away some of our ropes and making wind-holes through the sails. It was the work of a moment; the schooner luffed up under the lee of the brig, and, with almost the rapidity of thought, we were made fast to her main chains.

"Boarders away!" shouted Capt. S. We clambered up the sides of the brig, and dropped on board of her like so many locusts, not, however, till two of our lads were run through with boarding-pikes. The enemy made a brave defense, but were soon overpowered by superior numbers, and the captain of the brig was mortally wounded. In twenty minutes after we got alongside, the stars and stripes were waving triumphantly over the British flag. In this affair, we had two killed and seven slightly wounded, besides having some of our rigging cut away, and sails somewhat riddled.

The brig was from Jamaica, bound to the Gulf of Maracaibo; her cargo consisted of sugar, fruit, &c. She was two hundred tons' burden, mounted six six-pounders, with a complement of fifteen men, all told. She was manned with a prize-master and crew, and ordered to any port in the United States wherever she could get in.

This affair very much disgusted me with privateering, especially when I saw so much loss of life, and beheld a band of ruthless desperadoes—for such I must call our crew—robbing and plundering a few defenseless beings, who were pursuing both a lawful and peaceable calling. It induced me to form a resolve that I would relinquish what, to my mind, appeared to be an unjustifiable and outrageous pursuit; for I could not then help believing, that no conscientious man could be engaged in privateering, and certainly there was no honor to be gained by it.

The second lieutenant came to the same determination as myself; and both of us most cordially despised our commander, because it was with his permission that those most outrageous scenes of robbing and plundering were committed on board of the brig.

While refitting and resupplying in Cartagena, the *George Washington* met up with the *Black Joke* and both ships made preparations to return to the shipping lanes in search of English prey. The captain of the *George Washington*, however, proposed that they take sail under the Cartagena flag; the city had previously declared itself independent from the other Spanish colonies in the Caribbean.

This was a dangerous though potentially lucrative idea. Sailing under the flag of Cartagena would have meant that any vessel would be fair game, regardless of its national affiliation. This would mean that the privateering mission would come to an end and that they would, in effect, be nothing more than common pirates—a road that would lead directly to the gallows if the crew were ever seized by a foreign power. George Little and the second lieutenant of the *George Washington* managed to talk "Capt. S" out of the idea, saying that if that was a course he wished to chart, then he would be sailing alone. The risky endeavor was abandoned and the patriotic cause resumed, but the true avaricious nature of their captain had become clear to the officers of the *George Washington*. Joining forces with the *Black Joke*, they set sail once again, but more cautiously than when they had left Virginia.

While together, we captured several small British schooners, the cargoes of which, together with some spice, were divided between the two privateers. Into one of the prizes we put all the prisoners, gave them plenty of water and provisions, and let them pursue their course: the remainder of the prizes were burned. We then parted company, and, being short of water, ran in towards the land, in order to ascertain if any could be procured.

In approaching the shore, the wind died away to a perfect calm, and, at 4 P.M., a small schooner was seen in shore of us. As we had not steerage way upon our craft, of course it would be impossible to ascertain her character before dark; it was, therefore, determined by our commander to board her with the boats, under cover of the night. This was a dangerous service, but there was no backing out. Volunteers being called for, I stepped forward; and very soon, a sufficient number of men to man two boats offered their services to back me.

Every disposition was made for the attack. The men were strongly armed, oars muffled, and a grappling placed in each boat. The bearings of the strange sail were taken, and night came on perfectly clear and cloudless. I took command of the expedition, the second lieutenant having charge of one boat. The arrangement was to keep close together, until we got sight of the vessel; the second lieutenant was to board on the bow, and I on the quarter. We proceeded in the most profound silence; nothing was heard, save now and then a slight splash of the oars in the water, and before we obtained sight of the vessel I had sufficient time to reflect on this most perilous enterprise.

My reflections were not of the most pleasant character, and I found myself inwardly shrinking, when I was aroused by the voice of the bowman, saying, "There she is, sir, two points on the starboard bow." There she lay, sure enough, with every sail hoisted, and a light was distinctly seen, as we supposed, from her deck, it being too high for the cabin-windows. We now held a consultation, and saw no good reason to change the disposition of attack, except that we agreed to board simultaneously. It may be well to observe here, that any number of men on a vessel's deck, in the night, have double the advantage to repel boarders, because they may secrete themselves in such a position as to fall upon an enemy unawares, and thereby cut them off, with little difficulty.

Being fully aware of this, I ordered the men, as soon as we had gained the deck of the schooner, to proceed with great caution, and keep close together, till every hazard of the enterprise was ascertained. The boats now separated, and pulled for their respective stations, observing the most profound silence. When we had reached within a few yards of the schooner, we lay upon our oars for some moments, but could neither hear nor see any thing. We then pulled away cheerily, and the next minute were under her counter, and grappled to her; every man leaped on the deck without opposition. The other boat boarded nearly at the same moment, and we proceeded in a body, with great caution, to examine the decks. A large fire was in the caboose, and we soon ascertained that her deck was entirely deserted, and that she neither had any boat on deck, nor to her stern.

We then proceeded to examine the cabin, leaving an armed force on deck. The cabin, like the deck, being deserted, and the mystery was easily unraveled. Probably concluding that we should board them undercover of the night, they, no doubt, as soon as it was dark, took to their boats, and deserted the vessel.

Having successfully captured the abandoned vessel, Little took command and sailed her back to meet up with the others. They transferred any valuable cargo onto the *George Washington* and put a prize master in command of the new ship. While sailing back to rejoin the other ships, Little had steered a course through shallow waters along the nearby shoreline of the Rio de La Hache, where he spied a small settlement of huts. It had occurred to him that the settlement might be able to supply the ships with fresh water.

Little knew, however, that most of the natives in the settlements along the Rio de La Hache were exceedingly ferocious, and rumored to be cannibals. It was also well known that few who fell into the hands of these Indians ever escaped with their lives. While proposing his plan to approach the settlement for fresh water, Little suggested that it would be a wise precaution to see if they could lure some of the Indians out to sea with a decoy and hold them captive and hostage aboard the privateer as assurance against threat to the landing party attempting to acquire provisions. Upon hearing this recommendation, Capt. S accused George Little of cowardice and declared that if the lieutenant was too afraid of the natives to venture ashore, then he would himself undertake the mission. Little resolved to proceed with the undertaking.

The next morning, twenty water-casks were put on board the prize, together with the two boats and twenty men, well armed with muskets, pistols, and cutlasses, with a supply of ammunition; I repaired on board, got the prize under way, ran in, and anchored about one hundred yards from the beach. The boats were got in readiness, and the men were well armed, and the water-casks slung, ready to proceed on shore. I had examined my own pistols narrowly that morning, and had put them in complete order, and, as I believed, had taken every precaution for our future operations, so as to prevent surprise.

There were about a dozen ill-constructed huts, or wigwams . . . One solitary Indian was seen stalking on the beach, and the whole scene presented the most wild and savage appearance and, to my mind, augured very unfavorably. We pulled in with the casks in tow, seven men being in each boat; when within a short distance of the beach, the boats' heads were put to seaward, when the Indian came abreast of us. Addressing him in Spanish, I inquired if water could be procured, to which he replied in the affirmative. I then displayed to his view some gewgaws and trinkets, at which he appeared perfectly delighted, and, with many signs and gestures, invited me on shore.

Thrusting my pistols into my belt, and buckling on my cartridge-box, I gave orders to the boats' crews, that in case they discovered any thing like treachery or surprise, after I had gotten on shore, to cut the water-casks adrift, and make the best of their way on board the prize. As soon as I had jumped on shore, I inquired if there were any live stock, such as fowls, &c., to be had. Pointing to a hut about thirty yards from the boats, he said that the stock was there, and invited me to go and see it. I hesitated, suspecting some treachery; however, after repeating my order to the boats' crews, I proceeded with the Indian, and when within about half a dozen yards of the hut, at a prearranged signal, (as I supposed,) as if by magic, at least one hundred Indians rushed out, with the rapidity of thought. I was knocked down, stripped of all my clothing except an inside flannel shirt, tied hand and foot, and then taken and secured to the trunk of a large tree, surrounded by about twenty squaws, as a guard, who, with the exception of two or three, bore a most wild and hideous look in their appearance.

The capture of the boats' crews was simultaneous with my own, they being so much surprised and confounded at the stratagem of the Indians, that they had not the power, or presence of mind, to pull off. After they had secured our men, a number of them jumped into the boats, pulled off, and captured the prize, without meeting with any resistance from those on board—they being only six in number. Her cable was then cut, and she was run on the beach, when they proceeded to dismantle her, by cutting the sails from the bolt-ropes, and taking out what little cargo there was, consisting of Jamaica rum, sugar, &c.

This being done, they led ropes on shore from the schooner, when about one hundred of them hauled her up nearly high and dry. By this time the privateer had seen our disaster, stood boldly in, and anchored within less than gunshot of the beach; they then very foolishly opened a brisk cannonade, but every shot was spent in vain. This exasperated the Indians, and particularly the one who had taken possession of my pistols. Casting my eye around, I saw him creeping towards me with one pistol presented, and when about five yards off, he pulled the trigger. But as Providence had, no doubt, ordered it, the pistol snapped; at the same moment a shot from the privateer fell a few yards from us, when the Indian rose upon his feet, cocked the pistol, and fired it at the privateer; turning round with a most savage yell, he threw the pistol with great violence, which grazed my head, and then with a large stick beat and cut me until I was perfectly senseless.

This was about 10 o'clock, and I did not recover my consciousness until, as I supposed, about 4 o'clock in the afternoon. I perceived there were four squaws sitting around me, one of whom, from her appearance, (having on many gewgaws and trinkets) was the wife of a chief. As soon as she discovered signs of returning consciousness, she presented me with a gourd, the contents of which appeared to be Indian meal mixed with water; she first drank, and then gave it to me, and I can safely aver that I never drank any beverage, before or since, which produced such relief.

Night was now coming on; the privateer had got under way, and was standing off and on, with a flag of truce flying at her mast-head. The treacherous Indian with whom I had first conversed came, and, with a malignant smile, gave me the dreadful intelligence that at 12 o'clock that night we were to be roasted and eaten.

Accordingly, at sunset I was unloosed and conducted by a band of about half a dozen savages to the spot, where I found the remainder of our men firmly secured by having their hands tied behind them, their legs lashed together, and each man fastened to a stake that had been driven into the ground for that purpose. There was no possibility to elude the vigilance of these miscreants. As soon as night shut in, a large quantity of brushwood was piled around us, and nothing now was wanting but the fire to complete this horrible tragedy.

The same malicious savage approached us once more, and with the deepest malignity taunted us with our coming fate. Having some knowledge of the Indian character, I summoned up all the fortitude of which I was capable, and in terms of defiance told him that twenty Indians would be sacrificed for each one of us sacrificed by him. I knew very well that it would not do to exhibit any signs of fear or cowardice; and, having heard much of the cupidity of the Indian character, I offered the savage a large ransom if he would use his influence to procure our release. Here the conversation was abruptly broken off by a most hideous yell from the whole tribe, occasioned by their having taken large draughts of the rum, which now began to operate very sensibly upon them; and, as it will be seen, operated very much to our advantage.

George Little concluded that this would be his last night on Earth. He was convinced that he would be dead before dawn and sat terrified by the prospect of the slow and agonizing end, which awaited only the lighting of the fires at midnight. He thought of all of his friends and family members who had tried to persuade him through the years to settle into a stable profession and live a life of peace and comfort rather than taking to the uncertainty of the seas.

Fate, it would however seem, had other plans for him. When the Indians had rowed out to tow in the schooner, they had raided its stores. Within the hold among the Jamaican sugar and fruit were several large casks of strong rum. The Indians had been celebrating their own cleverness and good fortune by consuming as much of the rum as possible. As can often happen in the course of a raucous party, a fight had broken out among the drunken natives while the sailors waited to be roasted and eaten.

> Many of them lay stretched on the ground with tomahawks deeply implanted in their skulls; and many others, as the common phrase is, were "dead drunk." This was an exceedingly fortunate circumstance for us . . . With their senses benumbed, of course, they had forgotten their avowal to roast us . . . When the fumes of the liquor had in some degree worn off from the benumbed senses of the savages, they arose and approached us, and, for the first time, the wily Indian informed me that the tribe had agreed to ransom us. They then cast off the lashings from our bodies and feet, and, with our hands still secured, drove us before them to the beach.

The process of ransoming the captives to the captain of the *George Washington* was slow and complicated, but eventually all of the sailors were exchanged one or two at a time for trade goods, equipment, or cargo. Eventually, only Little remained and his ransom was set at more than double that of any of the other captives. Capt. S stalled and tried to negotiate a lesser settlement. Once an agreement had finally been reached, the trade was arranged only to be interrupted by another tribe arriving on the shore and wanting in on the action. The newcomers tried to capture George Little from his captors and intense fighting broke out on the beach. Little managed to escape in one of the longboats with Indians rowing after him in close pursuit until the privateer dramatically interposed itself and opened up with volleys of musket fire.

Little was none too happy with the captain following his narrow escape: "My dislike for the captain had very much increased since that unhappy, disastrous affair . . . I determined, therefore, in conjunction with the second lieutenant, to leave the privateer as soon as we arrived in Carthagena, to which port we were now bound."

Two days later, the privateers fell in with a Spanish schooner. The terms of their letters of marque were such that they were to attack any British ships or those of its allies who might be supplying the English with provisions. This ship, however, was Spanish, and as such was not involved in the conflict. Nevertheless, Captain S gave orders to attack the schooner. Little and the second lieutenant objected. The captain went to his cabin and retrieved a Cartagena flag and a commission. He hoisted the flag, and in a blatant act of piracy captured and looted the schooner.

All of the ships now made their way to the port of Cartagena where Little and the second lieutenant demanded their discharge and their shares of the prize money (amounting to eighteen hundred dollars each). Using those funds, the two officers purchased a fine schooner and succeeded in acquiring a commission to deliver freight and passengers to New Orleans.

We arrived at New Orleans, after a passage of eleven days, without accident or interruption. Here all was excitement, as the news of the capture of the Guerriere frigate by the Constitution had just been received.

Three large privateers were fitting out, from the commanders of which very tempting offers were thrown out to enter on board; but I had enough of privateering, and considered it at that time a most unjustifiable mode of warfare; and, although I could not obtain business for our vessel, and

the probability was that nothing would offer for some time,
I resolved to remain on shore rather than to engage again in
that nefarious calling.

While Little may have had lost his taste for privateering, he
quickly found life on land to be uncomfortable. New Orleans was a
very cosmopolitan and international port. It was full of strange ways
and foreign customs. Licentiousness, drunkenness, and lascivious
behavior were commonplace and not to the liking of the moralistic
George Little. He decided, therefore, to accept an offer to serve as
first officer of a privateering vessel bound for Bordeaux in France
and leaving on October 8, 1812.

This vessel was a schooner of three hundred tons' burden,
Baltimore-built, and of the most beautiful symmetrical proportions; she mounted ten guns, with a crew consisting of
thirty men. Our commander was a native of New Orleans, a
good seaman, possessing, at the same time, great affability of
manners and great decision of character. The second officer
was an old American seaman, rough in his exterior, yet, at
the same time, frank, open, and generous, with a frame and
constitution that seemed to defy the hardships of a sea life.
The crew were a fine set of able seamen, and in such a craft I
promised myself as much comfort as could be expected apart
from the danger of capture and the perils of the sea.
    Nothing material transpired until we reached the
Maranilla Reef [in the Florida Keys], when, on the morning
of the 21st, we fell in with an English frigate. Fortunately for
us, we were to the windward, or she would have crippled us,
being within gun-shot. All sail was made on the schooner;
the chase continued throughout the whole day . . . When
night set in, under its cover we altered our course, and eluded
the vigilance of the enemy, for in the morning nothing was
to be seen from the mast-head.

The French vessel escaped again as they approached the Outer
Banks, where they found themselves caught between two English

sloops of war. They loosed their sails and made a rapid escape. But the English ships gave chase for days until a storm blew up and they managed to lose their pursuers somewhere in the mid-Atlantic. They breathed a deep sigh of relief as they approached the European coastline, but then the wind died to a still calm and they drifted quietly and waited.

On the 13th of November, we were within half a day's sail of Bourdeaux, and fully expected, with a moderate breeze, to make Cordovan lighthouse early next morning. Alas! How soon are the brightest prospects frustrated! At sunset that evening, it fell away calm, and nothing was to be seen from the mast-head; not a breath of air or "cat's paw" was felt during the whole of the night. . . . When the morning dawn broke forth, conviction came, and suspense was at an end; for there lay a ship and two brigs, with English ensigns flying at their peaks. Flight was now impossible, for it was a dead calm; and resistance was entirely useless, for we lay at the mercy of their whole broadsides.

Our ensign was hoisted, but we well knew, to our great mortification, it must soon be hauled down in unresisting humility. The ship first opened her battery upon us, followed by one of the brigs. The rest is soon told. The American ensign was struck, and in twenty minutes they had possession of this valuable vessel and cargo. So strong was my presentiment of some coming disaster, that I had taken the precaution, during the night, to sew up in a flannel shirt all the money I had, consisting of seventeen doubloons, and then put it on. It was well I did so, for these vessels proved to be three Guernsey privateers.

After getting possession of the schooner, they robbed us of almost every thing they could lay their hands upon. Our crew were distributed among the three vessels; the captain, myself, and two men, were put on board the ship. The schooner was manned, and ordered to the Island of Guernsey; after which the privateers separated, to cruise on different stations. The destination of the ship, from what I understood, was to cruise on the coasts of Spain and Portugal.

The captain and myself received good treatment; for, after we had reported to the captain of the privateer the loss of our clothing, he ordered a search to be made for them, and all were recovered, as they happened to be on board of the ship. They were very much elated with their success, and assured us that the first licensed ship they fell in with, we should be released.

Three days after our capture, while standing on a wind, the cry of "Sail ho!" was heard from the mast-head, bearing on the lee beam. The ship was kept off, until the strange sail could be clearly made out. It proved to be a large rakish-looking schooner, evidently American by the set of her masts, cut of the sails, and color of the canvass. It was immediately suggested to us by the captain of the ship that there was another fine prize, and I was requested to look at her with the glass.

I soon discovered that she was a man-of-war of some description, and intimated as much to him; he was soon confirmed in this opinion, for the strange sail kept her wind, and manifested no disposition to get out of the way. When the ship had gotten within two miles of the schooner, she hauled her wind and made every preparation for action. . . . Night came on; and under its cover the course of the ship was altered, in order, if possible, to elude the one in pursuit. . . . It was a night of deep suspense to all, and especially to us. The captain of the ship was aware that the schooner would not engage in the night; consequently every advantage was taken of the wind to get clear of her, but it was all in vain. At daylight, in the morning, the schooner was about a mile astern.

Capt. N. and myself were now ordered below, when a running fight commenced, the ship discharging her stern-chasers in quick succession, and the schooner discharging her forward division, which cut away the stern boat and part of her starboard quarter. In half an hour the contest was decided, most of the ship's crew having deserted their quarters; the British flag was hauled down, and she became a prize to the Paul Jones privateer, of New York, mounting eighteen guns, with a complement of one hundred and twenty men. The boats immediately came from the privateer, and the crew of the ship was sent on board the schooner.

Now, a scene of plunder and robbery was perpetrated, by the privateer's crew, which beggars all description; every article of clothing and stores, which they could lay their hands upon, were taken without any ceremony. The crew were a perfect set of desperadoes and outlaws, whom the officers could neither restrain nor command.

Capt. N. and myself were now conveyed to the privateer without our clothes, for we had shared the like fate with the crew of the ship, by having our trunks broken open and robbed of all their contents.

The excitement being over, a prize-master and crew were put on board of the ship, and she was ordered to the United States. Capt. N. prevailed with the captain of the privateer to let him proceed in her; but all the arguments I could make use of, to accompany him, were fruitless; so I concluded to make the best of a bad bargain, and was induced, by the persuasions of the captain and the prospect of gain held out to me, to enter as prize-master.

Thus it was that the honorable and earnest sailor remembered by history as George Little, merchant captain of Baltimore, took to privateering for patriotic causes against the might of the British navy—only to end up nearly becoming a cannibal's banquet, turn momentary pirate, get captured by the English off the coast of France, and then, while sailing on that English ship, be taken captive in turn by American privateers who would eventually return him home to Maryland.

Joshua Barney and the Battle of Bladensburg

Since the 1980 discovery of a sunken ship that was once a part of the Chesapeake Flotilla, Marylanders have become much more aware of the sinking of the flotilla and the subsequent Battle of Bladensburg, both of which occurred in Prince George's County. As a result of the discovery, one of the ships that served as part of the flotilla has been reconstructed and launched. This craft, a copy of the barge used by Joshua Barney, helps bring back to life incidents that formed two of the most pivotal events in the War of 1812.

Eight months after President James Madison declared war against Great Britain in June 1812, a fleet of Royal Navy warships entered the Chesapeake and began a campaign of unrestrained warfare against the communities of the Maryland and Virginia tidewater. The U.S. Navy, blockaded in the Elizabeth River by the British Royal Navy, was unable to provide protection for the beleaguered farms and villages of the region. While America was being pummeled by British land and naval forces, retired Commodore Barney was on his farm in Anne Arundel County. Although he had once been the youngest captain in the United States Navy and a genuine naval hero of the Revolutionary War, he was now in his mid-fifties. A successful shipping merchant, he was never far from the sea, and had volunteered his services to President Madison as early as 1809, asking to be "employed in any manner which might be thought conducive to the good of my country."

After observing with frustration the unsuccessful political, legal, and military actions being taken by his government against the invading British, Barney submitted his own war plan to powerful friends in Maryland's legislature and the U.S. War Department.

The commodore's audacious plan became all the more imperative when British rear admiral Sir George Cockburn reappeared in Lynnhaven Bay (now Virginia Beach) in early March 1814 to carry out the instructions of his commanding officer Admiral Alexander Cochrane "to devastate and ravage the seaport towns." At about the same time, the sensational news that Napoleon had been defeated was received from France. His defeat released thousands of tough British veterans for service elsewhere—presumably on this side of the Atlantic. Spurred into action by this increased threat, the American government funded the construction of a fleet of row galleys and military authorities and granted state governments the right "to recruit men for the Chesapeake Flotilla . . . to serve in the defense of the Chesapeake and its tidelands." Simultaneously, the retired Commodore Joshua Barney was given a new commission as a "Captain in the Flotilla Service of the United States," signed by President Madison on April 25, 1814.

A ship builder as well as a fighter, Barney turned a hurriedly assembled fleet of eighteen scows and barges into gunboats complete with cannons and manned by 503 seamen. On May 24, Barney's fleet sailed out of Baltimore harbor with the intent of taking on the indomitable fleet of the honorable Admiral Sir George Cockburn. Barney's initial target was the main British naval base on Tangier Island in the Chesapeake Bay.

Obviously he could not challenge Cockburn's heavyweights ship-for-ship. But he knew the Chesapeake—its deep water, its shoals, its numerous shallow creeks and estuaries into which he could find safety. So, like all able commanders, Barney adjusted his tactics to his terrain and his strength and became a waterborne gadfly. He buzzed, rather than assaulted, the enemy. He would wait until a likely victim came too close to his watery sanctuaries and his flotilla, led by his appropriately named flagship, the sloop-of-war USS *Scorpion*, which had eight carronades and one long gun, plus a furnace for heating shot. Leaping out of hiding whenever the enemy came within reach, Barney would inflict as much damage on them as he could and then retreat. He never hoped to sink their ships, but he certainly made Sir George Cockburn pay attention.

On June first, the flotilla encountered the British schooner HMS *St. Lawrence* and seven companion boats, sailing between the mouths of the Potomac and Patuxent Rivers near Cedar Point. In what became known as the Battle of Cedar Point, the barges pursued the British, firing away, until the beleaguered schooner came under the protection of the huge seventy-four-gun line-of-battle ship HMS *Dragon*. When the *Dragon*'s big guns opened up, Barney's gunboats turned around and ran for shallow water, with the big British ship lumbering in futile pursuit. Because of Barney, Cockburn's hopes of renewing the previous year's campaign of pillage and plunder were frustrated; instead of repeating such atrocities like the burning of the town of Havre de Grace, Maryland, his forces were reduced to pig rustling and tobacco stealing.

Thus began a series of darting attacks, frantic retreats and tardy reinforcements that culminated in the entire Chesapeake Flotilla being blocked inside the confines of the Patuxent River.

On June 7, the flotilla retreated up the Patuxent River and moved two miles upstream beyond St. Leonard's Creek. The mouth of the creek was blockaded by two British frigates: the thirty-eight-gun HMS *Loire* and the thirty-two-gun HMS *Narcissus*, plus the sloop-of-war HMS *Jasseur* with eighteen guns. For three days the British Navy launched wave after wave of assaults against the U.S. forces, often employing Congreve rockets to destroy the flotilla, but the commodore and his men stood fast. On each occasion the small British boats and launches came upstream until they caught sight of Barney's flotilla before they were promptly chased off by the Americans, who always took care not to meddle with the larger vessels.

Colonel Decius Wadsworth, commanding a force of American artillery on shore, offered to coordinate his efforts with the flotilla's attack on the two frigates. Assisted by a force of U.S. Marines commanded by a Captain Miller, the joint attack took place on June 26. As the story goes, Commodore Barney gave this simple command to his men when they rowed into battle: "Sails and oars!" (Full speed ahead.) Imagine rowing into battle in a barge manned by heavy oars twenty feet in length and weighing 38 pounds—a nearly impossible task, accomplished by the hands and efforts of fearless patriots and their special kind of leader. The *Loire* and *Narcissus* remained largely undamaged but they were driven off, and the flotilla rowed triumphantly into the Patuxent.

President Madison received word on July 1 that a fleet of British troop transports with a large military force was about to leave Bermuda, bound for an unknown port in the United States, probably on the Potomac. The District of Columbia formed part of the Fourth Military District, in which the effective troops, under Brigadier General William H. Winder, numbered about two thousand, scattered over widely separated points; some were as far away from Washington as Norfolk, Virginia. A single company of marines was stationed at the barracks in Washington, and a company of artillery was at Fort Washington. General Winder had warned the government that imminent peril threatened and had asked for troops with which to meet it, but it seemed impossible to convince the authorities that he was right, or that any circumstances could arise that would place the capital in peril. General Winder was personally convinced that Annapolis was the real British objective, but most other military and government officials believed that Baltimore was the British destination.

For unknown reasons, no effective measures were taken to put the national capital in a state of defense. Fort Washington, a few miles below the city on the Maryland side of the Potomac, could offer some resistance to ships but there was a nearly unobstructed route to the capital through Maryland from the Chesapeake and up the Patuxent River. Commodore Barney was called to Washington in July for consultation with the Secretary of the Navy, William Jones, "in regard to the protection of that capital." The secretary warned Barney that the threat against the captial might be "a feint, to mask a real design on Baltimore."

In mid-August a large portion of the Royal Naval fleet, commanded by Admiral Cockburn, and four thousand veteran soldiers known as "Wellington's Invincibles," under the command of Major General Robert Ross, made their appearance in the Chesapeake, escalating an already desperate situation. To counter this threat, Commodore Barney moved his flotilla up the Patuxent as far as Nottingham, about forty miles from Washington, where he reported to the Navy Department that the enemy had entered and were ascending the river. "The British are in the Patuxent," Commodore Barney wrote Navy Secretary Jones on Friday, August 19. The admiral, he was told, planned to destroy Barney's flotilla and "dine in Washington on Sunday." Secretary Jones ordered Barney to run his flotilla as far up the river as possible, and when the enemy landed, to destroy the flotilla and then march to join General Winder.

On August 19 and 20, the British divisions landed at Benedict, Maryland, and marched along the Patuxent River while their ships kept pace with them, offering support. The advancing British troops numbered five thousand, including one thousand Royal Marines.

Following his orders, Barney retreated upriver to about five miles north of Pig Point. There he landed with four hundred men, leaving about a hundred men to blow up the flotilla. On the morning of August 22, the British were astounded to see an orderly line of American rowing galleys and merchant ships blocking the river in front of them. They were far more surprised when the American ships blew up in quick succession. More than sixteen ships of the Chesapeake Flotilla sank in the Patuxent in a matter of minutes, effectively blocking the channel.

General Winder's militia were scattered across miles of open country and he found himself left with only five hundred regulars and two thousand undisciplined militia, made up mostly of farmers armed only with shotguns. With this force he was expected to counter a major landing force of the best-trained soldiers on Earth. On August 22, Winder learned that the British had camped the previous night at Nottingham, leading him to conclude that they were indeed heading for Washington rather than Baltimore or Annapolis.

Winder knew that a sizable British naval force was proceeding up the Potomac, and feared that they would be joined by the ground troops to attack Fort Washington, an easy westward march from Nottingham. Attacking across the bridge over the Eastern Branch of the Potomac (now the Anacostia) at Bladensburg seemed a fairly remote possibility. Winder's scouts continued to report on the activities of the British, who were now in Upper Marlboro. One report said they were on the road to Annapolis; another that they were heading for Fort Washington; another that they were again on the road towards Bladensburg.

At ten o'clock on the morning of August 24, a scout came galloping into the general's camp with news that the British had been marching for Bladensburg since dawn and were nearly halfway there. Preparing for the coming engagement, General Winder organized his forces to cover the road west of town, on the west bank of the Eastern Branch of the Potomac. This put them in a good position to defend the bridge over which the British soldiers would be forced to pass.

Notified of these developments by Winder, Commodore Barney's little band of 370 men proceeded by forced march to Bladensburg, accompanied by Captain Samuel Miller, 120 U.S. Marines, and five pieces of heavy artillery scavenged from the flotilla and the Washington Navy Yard. Barney arrived at 1 P.M., at the same time the British began attacking Winder's forward line. Barney arranged his artillery in battery formation at the center of Winder's second-line position. The commodore himself directed the artillery (two eighteen-pound and three twelve-pound ship's guns mounted on carriages), while Captain Miller commanded the rest of the force.

The two first attacks of the British were bloodily repulsed, chiefly by Barney's guns. Barney recounted:

> At length the enemy made his appearance on the main road in force and in front of my battery, and on seeing us made a halt. I reserved our fire. In a few minutes the enemy again advanced, when I ordered an 18-pounder to be fired, which completely cleared the road. Shortly after, a second and a

third attempt was made by the enemy to come forward, but all were destroyed. They then crossed over into an open field, and attempted to flank our right. He was met there by three 12-pounders, and Marines under Captain Miller, and my men acting as infantry, and again was totally cut up. By this time not a vestige of the American army remained, except a body of five or six hundred posted on a height on my right, from which I expected much support from their fine position.

As the British attempted a flanking movement, Barney ordered Captain Miller and the infantry to charge, while his cannon pounded the enemy flanks. The charge was beautifully executed and the British 86th and 4th divisions, known as the "King's Own Regiment," were forced to retreat. Pursued by the American sailors crying out to "board 'em," the British were driven into a wooded ravine, leaving several wounded officers in the hands of the Americans. Colonel William Thornton, who bravely led the attacking British column, was severely wounded, and General Ross had his horse shot out from under him.

Commodore Barney's heroic resistance prevented the battle of Bladensburg from ending in an unqualified disgrace for America. It was a magnificent stand; the slightest follow-up of Barney's counter-attack might have produced an American victory. However, the opportunity was lost through lack of manpower and lack of organization. Because of the absence of support troops the British were able to take up positions on Barney's flanks, where they regrouped and opened fire on the Americans. Several of Barney's best men were killed or wounded. Captain Miller had been wounded in charging the enemy, and Commodore Barney himself, after having had his horse killed under him, received a musket ball in the thigh.

The only hope the Americans had of maintaining their tenuous position was for their own relief troops to arrive before British reinforcements. As British numbers and strength grew, Winder was forced to order a general retreat. But somehow, in the confusion and terror of the losing battle, the retreat order never reached Commodore Barney. Now with almost no powder or ammunition, a rapidly increasing number of enemy troops on his right flank, and no support on his left, Barney had no alternative but to order his troops to spike their cannon and retreat as quickly as possible to a safe position. The road to Washington now lay open. Because of his wounded leg, Barney could not be moved; he was taken prisoner by the advancing British.

Despite having lost nearly three hundred men and several of his best officers in his assault on the American positions, British general Ross treated Barney with all the respect and care his rank demanded. Like Barney, Ross was an honorable soldier and recognized another good soldier when he saw one. In an astonishing act of chivalry Ross immediately pardoned Commodore Barney, along with all of his flotilla men, and provided an escorted wagon to move Barney into Washington so he could have his leg properly attended to.

The War of 1812 ended as quickly as it began. In December 1814, only three months after the Battle of Bladensburg, representatives of America and the British Empire signed peace terms in Ghent, Belgium. Not long after his recovery, the city of Washington presented a commemorative sword to Commodore Joshua Barney. On its blade are inscribed the words: "In testimony of the intrepidity and valor of Commodore Joshua Barney, and the handful of men under his immediate command in the defense of the City of Washington on the twenty-fourth of August, 1814."

Captain Thomas Boyle of Fells Point

In 1730, William Fell, a recent arrival from England, chose an eighty-acre tract of land southeast of Baltimore Town in Maryland Colony as the perfect location for his shipyard and home. The land had ample trees to provide lumber, there were iron foundries nearby, and the natural harbor's depth was ideal for building and launching his two-masted ships.

Forty-three years later, Baltimore annexed the area and William's son, Edward, laid out a town he christened Fells Point. The streets had names like Thames and Shakespeare. The alleys included Strawberry, Apple, Happy, and Petticoat. With a promising future ahead, other shipwrights and associated industries began to arrive, and when the fledging American nation needed ships for her navy, the government opted to have two of them, the *Wasp* and the *Hornet*, built at Fells Point. Between June 1776 and May 1778, 224 letters of marque were issued to Maryland-registered privateer vessels. The last such commission granted to an American vessel during the Revolutionary War was given to a Maryland schooner.

Between the war's end and 1797, nearly sixty thousand tons of commerce passed through Baltimore. By 1800 the city was the third largest in the United States, a rank it held until 1830. But what drew ship owners, their captains, and sailors to this thriving port was its reputation for building fast, sleek vessels.

Between 1795 and 1835 the most popular style of craft built at the Fells Point shipyards was the Baltimore schooner. The displacement of these ships averaged 116 tons and their keels ranged from twenty-five feet to nearly one hundred feet in length, with an average length of fifty-nine feet. All of the Fells Point schooners carried at least two masts and all were fore- and aft-rigged. (For more details see "schooner" and "rigging" in the glossary). During this period a total of 421 schooners were built at Fells Point in shipyards owned by eighty-three different master shipwrights.

One of these nautical master craftsmen was a young Quaker from the Eastern Shore who arrived in Baltimore around 1803. His name was Thomas Kemp and over his career he would build an impressive total of fifty-two vessels—thirty-nine of which were schooners. Kemp purchased land at the northeast corner of Market (now Broadway) and Lancaster Streets in Fells Point in December 1803. In August of that year, he had married Sophia Horstman. Before her death at the age of twenty-one in 1809, she gave birth to three children: Thomas H., Elizabeth, and Sophia. Later that year, Thomas remarried. He and his wife, the widowed Eliza Doyle, would have six children.

At first, Thomas probably worked in one of the shipyards, but by June 1804, he and his brother Joseph struck out on their own repairing existing vessels. Between other jobs the brothers built their own ship, the schooner *Thomas and Joseph*. Until 1805, however, they mostly repaired vessels.

On July 6, 1805, Thomas purchased a piece of property in Fells Point and established his own shipyard. Thomas employed about two dozen men, most of whom were carpenters and caulkers, and he described the vessels they built as "round tuck privateer fashion schooners." One of the first vessels built in the new yard was a ninety-nine-ton schooner named *Lynx*. Kemp developed a reputation for building high-quality boats known for their durability and speed. No other Baltimore shipwright of the period matched his genius. He built the four most successful privateer schooners used in the War of 1812: the *Rossie, Rolla, Comet,* and *Chasseur.*

Most, if not all, Baltimore schooners of this period had one deck and two masts. Speed was essential in their design, as was a shallow draft. The cogs of the Middle Ages had averaged six and one-half knots, and that speed didn't change much in the intervening years. John Paul Jones's famous Revolutionary War ship, the *Bonhomme Richard*, had a cruising speed of between five and seven knots. But the sharply raked (set at a greater angle than normal) masts of Baltimore schooners allowed them to use the wind more efficiently, as did the addition of topmasts, topsail yards, and topgallant yards. These vessels could cruise at speeds of up to eleven or twelve knots—an astonishing speed in the age of wooden ships and sails and still impressive for the most modern mid-sized sailcraft. The design features that made these ships sleek and fast also made them difficult to sail, especially in rough seas. A Baltimore schooner required a highly competent crew, usually consisting of less than 150 men, and a captain with good leadership skills to command the ship at her fastest speeds.

The speed of the Baltimore schooners baffled their pursuers and made the vessels objects of nautical curiosity. When captured, Baltimore schooners were sometimes brought into British navy yards, where sailors and captains inexperienced in the handling of such creations tried unsuccessfully to sail them. Considering the Royal Navy's boast that it had the most disciplined sailors in the world, this must have been truly frustrating.

At the start of the War of 1812, the American navy consisted of about seventeen vessels, the largest of which carried a total of fifty-six guns. The British Royal Navy, on the other hand, had significantly more and larger ships and far greater firepower. To compensate for this lack of firepower, the American government issued letters of marque to privateers.

Within six months, forty-two Baltimore vessels had privateering commissions. These privateers were armed with a total of 330 guns and carried three thousand men. It's estimated that before the end of the eighteen-month-long war a total of 185 Baltimore privateers carried letters of marque, a number sufficient to do significant damage to British trade and military actions. Occasionally, the privateers even captured Royal Navy vessels. The *Dash*, which hailed from Baltimore, carried only one gun when she captured the first enemy naval vessel, the four-gun cutter-schooner HMS *Whiting*.

The *Comet*, whose keel was sixty-eight-feet long and beam (width at the widest point) was twenty-three feet, was nearly 165 tons displacement. She cost $3,630, but her owner, Captain William Furlong, only had $1,505 and a Captain Thorndike Chase is recorded as having paid the balance. During the *Comet*'s third voyage, she captured an astounding twenty enemy vessels. One Englishman called her captain, Thomas Boyle, a "crazy American privateersman who wouldn't take no for an answer."

The finances involved in shipbuilding were always burdensome and numerous partners often combined their money to build a ship. Shipbuilder Thomas Kemp often owned shares in the privateer ships that were built in his shipyard. One such vessel, the *Chasseur*, mentioned earlier, was built as a merchant vessel for William Hollins and launched on December 12, 1812, as a topsail schooner. Her keel measured 85.66 feet, her breadth was twenty-six feet, and she had a displacement of nearly 296 tons. Sadly, as a merchant ship she was a dismal failure, partly because of her limited cargo space and also because the British blockade of the port of Baltimore and the Chesapeake Bay prevented her from ever reaching the open sea. After several weeks of tacking aimlessly off Annapolis, she returned to Baltimore. A second try was made, but her crew mutinied, and she limped home with just her captain and two or three sailors aboard.

Mercantile trading may have become impossible for *Chasseur*, but she was one of the fastest ships ever built, so her owners decided to sail her as a privateer. Privateering commission number 665 was granted to the *Chasseur* on February 23, 1813, and under the command of William Wade, she captured eleven vessels. They broke through the British blockade on Christmas Day 1813, and six months later put in at New York after a successful cruise. While in port, she was sold to a group of investors that included her builder, Thomas Kemp. They refitted her, replaced her carronades with sixteen long twelve-pounder cannons. When she passed Sandy Hook to begin her second cruise in July 1814, she also had a new captain, Thomas Boyle, who was one of the brig's owners and who had previously commanded the *Comet*, with the *Chasseur*'s last captain, William Wade serving as second officer.

Boyle was a true seaman; he had been at sea since the age of ten and was master of a ship by his sixteenth birthday. Three years later, he made Baltimore his home, although he had been born in Marblehead, Massachusetts. Boyle ran a tight ship, but had the respect of his crew. He drilled them over and over again in handling the sails and firing the sixteen guns *Chasseur* carried until it became second nature to them. Captain Boyle's insistence on daily drills allowed the sailors to become familiar with the idiosyncrasies of the guns, to practice with the tools of their trade, and to become so familiar with loading and firing that they could do so without thinking about their actions. The gunners had a variety of ammunition to choose from when loading a gun. They used round shot to smash a ship's hull and topple her masts. Chain shot damaged the rigging and swept the deck clear of crewmen. Bar shot devastated rigging and sails. Some guns were mounted on bed carriages with trucks. Others, called swivel guns, were mounted on a vessel's rails and used against an enemy crew like shotguns. During Boyle's command as a captain of privateers, he and his men captured somewhere between thirty and sixty ships. Three-fourths of his men were literate enough to sign their names to the articles of agreement under which they sailed.

Thomas Boyle was not only clever and courageous, but also audacious and bold. For three months, the *Chasseur* sailed through the English Channel and along the coasts of Britain and Ireland, capturing eighteen prizes. To the captain of one of these prizes, he gave a proclamation that he instructed the man to post at the London Coffee House of Lloyd's insurance company. It read:

BY THOMAS BOYLE, ESQUIRE; COMMANDER OF THE PRIVATE ARMED BRIG <u>CHASSEUR</u>

Whereas, it has been customary with the admirals of Great Britain commanding small forces on the coast of the

United States, particularly with Sir John Borlase Warren and Sir Alexander Cochrane to declare the coast of the said United States in a state of rigorous blockade, without possessing the power to justify such a declaration, or stationing an adequate force to command such a blockade.

I do, therefore, by virtue of the power and authority in me vested (possessing sufficient force) declare all the ports, harbors, bays, creeks rivers, inlets, outlets, island and sea coast of the United Kingdom of Great Britain and Ireland in a state of strict and rigorous blockade, and I do further declare that I consider the forces under my command adequate to maintain strictly, rigorously and effectually, the said blockade.

And, I do hereby require the respective officers, whether captains or commanding officers, under my command, employed or to be employed on the coast of England, Ireland and Scotland, to pay strict attention to this my proclamation.

And, I hereby caution and forbid the ships and vessels and every nation, in amity and peace with the United States, from entering or attempting to come out of any of the said ports, harbors, bays, creeks, rivers, inlets, islands, or sea coasts, on or under my pretense whatever; and that no person may plead ignorance of this my proclamation, I have ordered the same to be made public in England.

Given under my hand on board the Chasseur. By the commanding Officer, THOMAS BOYLE, J.B. STANSBURY, SECRETARY.

Forty years after the war, George Coggeshall, a fellow captain of privateers, wrote of Boyle: "He evidently possessed many of the elements of a great man, for in him were blended the impetuous bravery of a Murat, with the prudence of a Wellington. He wisely judged when to attack the enemy and when to retreat, with honor to himself and to the flag under which he sailed."

During her cruise, the *Chasseur* took the brig *Eclipse*, which had fourteen guns; the *Commerce,* another brig with a copper hull; the schooner *Fox*; three additional brigs, the *Antelope*, the *Marquis of Cornwallis*, and the *Atlantic*; and an eight-gun ship called *James*. Boyle also had his men burn several Scottish vessels. They skirmished with a frigate, pummeling her with two broadsides. The frigate fired a twenty-four-pound shot that struck the *Chasseur*'s foremast and "cut it nearly a third off." Another shot "struck the gunwale of port No. 5, tore away all the sill and plank shear" and unseated the gun before crashing through the deck and wounding three men, including a sailor named Henry Watson, who was "compelled to have his thigh amputated."

But each ship that Boyle took meant that he had to subdivide his crew so that the prize could be manned; captured ships not only depleted the enemy's fleet but, if brought back to port, provided valuable profit for the privateer's investors. Of his eighteen prizes, Boyle sent nine back to the States. When he had only sixty men left on the *Chasseur*, he sailed back to New York, arriving there on October 29, 1814. A Baltimore newspaper editor printed that *Chasseur*'s two successful cruises proved that the best way to win the war was to attack British commerce. He considered American sailors "the admiration of Europe and the terror of England." The success of Boyle and other American privateers severely affected the morale of British merchants and caused their insurance rates to skyrocket. In Halifax, a thirty-three percent surcharge was added to rates. Some underwriters refused to even insure the ships and their cargoes.

Before Boyle and the *Chasseur* returned to sea following his triumphant return to Baltimore, alterations were done to allow the vessel to convert it from brig to brigantine rigging. Boyle also replaced ten of the long twelve-pounders with carronade guns, which hit harder, used less powder, and were easier to load. The *Chasseur* returned to the hunt on December 23, 1814, shortly before the war ended. She exchanged shots with several enemy vessels and escaped from either a frigate or first-rate ship-of-the-line before engaging in her final battle.

News of the peace treaty which formally ended the war—signed on Christmas Eve 1814—had not reached Boyle when he sighted a new target on February 26, 1815. At the time, the *Chasseur* carried one hundred and two men and fourteen guns; Boyle had ordered the rest of his long guns dumped overboard to lighten the brig's load during a squall. The *Chasseur*'s opponent, HMS *St. Lawrence*, was sighted about thirty-six miles from Havana, Cuba, at eleven o'clock in the morning. This large, pilot-built schooner "with yellow sides" had been built in Philadelphia and christened *Atlas*, but had been captured by the English in Ocracoke Inlet, North Carolina. She was commandeered for use by the Royal Navy and carried a complement of seventy-six men and thirteen guns. Her captain was Lieutenant J. C. Gordon.

Thinking the enemy was a merchant vessel because he saw only three gun ports, Boyle attempted to close and board her, but the *Chasseur* was sailing too fast and shot under the *St. Lawrence*'s lee. The schooner greeted the American by revealing "a tier of ten ports in a side," but the soldiers and marines aboard remained hidden under the bulwark. The two vessels exchanged broadsides when they were only thirty feet apart. The battle continued for fifteen minutes before the British vessel struck her colors. The *St. Lawrence*'s masts toppled after the fighting ended, and her hull and spars were so damaged that Boyle sent her and her wounded crewmen to Cuba. He described her as "a perfect wreck in her hull and had scarcely a Sail or Rope standing." The damage to *Chasseur*, on the other hand, was mostly confined to her rigging and rails. Of the battle, Boyle recorded, "At this time both fires were very severe and destructive and we found we have an heavy enemy to contend with . . . Saw the blood run freely from her scuppers. Gave orders for boarding which was cheerfully obeyed." He reported casualties as fifteen killed and nineteen wounded for the British and five killed and nineteen wounded for the Americans.

Boyle also explained why he chose to fight rather than flee: "I should not willingly perhaps have sought a contest with a king's vessel knowing it was not our object, but my expectations were at first a valuable vessel and a valuable cargo. When I found myself deceived, the honor of the flag left with me was not to be disgraced by flight."

When Boyle met with the *St. Lawrence*'s skipper, Lt. Gordon, the Englishman gave him a letter, part of which said:

In the event of Captain Boyle's becoming a prisoner of war to any British cruiser I consider it a tribute justly due to his humane and generous treatment of myself, the surviving officers, and crew of His Majesty's late schooner *St. Lawrence,* to state that his obliging attention and watchful solicitude to preserve our effects and render us comfortable during the short time we were in his possession were such as justly entitle him to the indulgence and respect of every British subject.

In early or mid-March, a fellow American vessel out of Boston passed along news of peace. In late March or early April (sources vary on the date), the *Chasseur* sailed up the Patapsco River past Fort McHenry, which saluted her, into Baltimore. Hezekiah Niles, the editor of the *Niles' Register,* wrote:

She is, perhaps, the most beautiful vessel that ever floated in the ocean, those who have not seen our schooners have but little idea of her appearance. As you look at her you may easily figure to yourself the idea that she is about to rise out of the water and fly in the air, seeming to set so lightly upon it!

This newspaper also dubbed her "the Pride of Baltimore." She had captured twenty-three vessels under Boyle's leadership, and the proceeds from the sales of those plundered cargoes totaled $33,173.62. Boyle earned more than thirty thousand dollars from his cruises as captain and part-owner of the *Comet* and *Chasseur.*

After the war, Thomas Kemp, who had built the mighty *Chasseur,* returned to the Eastern Shore to live at his farm, Wade's Point. Five years later, he sold his Fells Point property, which included "a Very Comfortable and Roomy 2 story frame Dwelling house, a good brick Kitchen and Smoke house, A large work shop and very good counting house." Kemp died on March 3, 1824, at the age of forty-five, and was buried at Wade's Point.

The *Chasseur* was returned to her original purpose and again became a merchant vessel and sailed to China. After she was sold to foreign owners in 1816, she disappeared from the historical record. Boyle returned to commanding merchant ships, primarily in the

West Indies. He died at sea in 1825. The first notice of his death appeared in Philadelphia's *U.S. Gazette* on October 21.

> Captain Boyle was one of the oldest & most respectable ship masters out of the port of Baltimore; possessing a generous disposition, & a nobleness of mind, blending the polished gentleman with that of the sailor made him the favorite of all who knew him.

His estate was valued at about $10,051, and during the Second World War, the United States named a destroyer in his honor.

Following the War of 1812, shipbuilding and commerce almost halted in Fells Point. The reasons for this were numerous: inflation, outbreaks of yellow fever, and too many decommissioned privateers. Not until the launch of the *Ann McKim*, in 1833, did the first signs of recovery appear. From 1840 to 1895, Fells Point once again became a thriving seaport, this time supplying the vessels that became known as Baltimore clippers. (This name did not refer to the privateers that sailed during the War of 1812. They were often referred to then as "Baltimore Flyers.")

Once steamships took the place of sailing ships, other sections of Baltimore, like Locust Point, became the ports of choice because the water at Fells Point wasn't deep enough for the iron ships. Her shipyards closed and lumber, canning, and packing companies bought the abandoned properties. With the influx of new industries came immigrants who lived and worked there. Many of the original houses were razed during the first few decades of the 20th century, but eventually citizens petitioned for Fells Point to be declared a historic district. The area became the first National Registered Historic District in Maryland in 1969. Today visitors to this old seaport will find museums, shops, galleries, and restaurants as they walk the cobbled streets along the harbor—not to mention the annual Fells Point Privateer Festival.

Glossary

Barquentine   Barque

Barkentine (barquentine) and bark (barque). The barkentine and bark were both medium-size, three-masted ships generally ranging between 120 and 160 feet in length. The barkentine was distinguished from the bark in that the front (fore) mast of the barkentine was square rigged, and the two rear masts were fore-and-aft rigged. When the same type of ship had the fore mast and middle (main) mast rigged with square sails and only the rear mast fore-and-aft rigged, it was referred to as a bark. Larger and heavier than either the sloop or schooner, the barkentine was capable of carrying more and heavier cannons, but its size made it slower than these other ships. The barkentine's size and weight also made it unsuitable for shallow inlets and river navigation. Designed as a merchant vessel, this ship could be converted for military or privateer use when rigged with fore-and-aft sails.

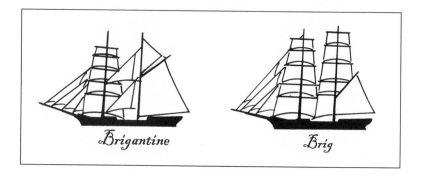

Brigantine   Brig

Brigantine and brig. The brigantine and brig were identical in
structure, two-masted ships ranging between 110 and 140 feet in
length and requiring a crew of 100 to 150 men to operate. The
difference in designation between the two was the sail arrangement. When set with square rigging on the front (fore) mast and
fore-and-aft rigging on the rear mast, the ship was referred to as
a brigantine; when set with square rigging on both masts and a
single fore-and-aft sail running behind the rear mast, it became
a brig. Both versions were popular as trading vessels, and both
were used for military purposes, with the brig rigging being the
more popular arrangement for military use. A fully armed brig
or brigantine could carry up to twenty 32-pounder cannons.
Smaller, faster, and lighter than either the man-of-war or ship-
of-the-line, the brig was an ideal pursuit vessel for chasing
pirates and privateers.

Cannon. Whereas modern cannons are measured in caliber, seven-
teenth- and eighteenth-century cannons were measured according
to the weight of the balls they fired. For instance, a six-pounder
cannon fired balls weighing six pounds. Eighteenth-century naval
cannons generally came in eight sizes: six-, nine-, twelve-, eight-
een-, twenty-four-, thirty-two-, forty-two-, and two hundred-
pounders. The balls ranged in diameter from 3.67 inches for the
six-pounder to 8 inches for the two hundred-pounder.

Cannon, naval. Although the barrels of naval cannons were similar
in size and weight to field cannons, the carriages on which they
were mounted were much lower than those of cannons used in
field battles. The wheels on which the beds rested were normally
no more than eight to twelve inches in diameter.

Frigate

Corvette. A corvette was a two-masted sloop converted for military or privateer use and rigged with a combination of square and fore-and-aft sails. Corvettes tended to be between forty and sixty feet in length. They were lightly armed with any number of swivel guns and six to eighteen lightweight cannons, all of which were mounted on the main deck. Fast, light, and easy to maneuver, the corvette was ideal for privateers and coastal patrols.

Cutter. Similar to the sloop in appearance, the cutter was a single-masted vessel that differed from the sloop only in that its single mast was located farther back on the ship. For further information, see *sloop*.

Frigate. A medium-size, three-masted, square-rigged warship, the frigate was smaller than the man-of-war and carried fewer cannons. Frigates tended to be 180 to 220 feet long and 46 to 50 feet wide, with an average below-the-waterline depth of 20 feet. The frigate's complement of twenty-eight to sixty cannons was located on its single gun deck, located directly below the upper deck. Under the direction of a skilled captain, a frigate could maneuver almost as well as a schooner and run faster than the sleekest merchant ship of the day. Frigates were first brought into service in 1757 by Britain's Royal Navy, which had sixty frigates by the time of the American Revolution.

Grapeshot. Grapeshot refers to small, round iron balls that could be fired from cannons as antipersonnel shot. They were similar in size to musket balls, about three-quarters of an inch in diameter. Grapeshot was usually banded together for ease of loading into the gun. When the gun was fired, the band would snap, allowing the shot to spread out for maximum dispersion.

Man of War

Letter of marque. A letter of marque was an official document issued by a government to a private citizen, giving the recipient and those in his employ the right to seize or destroy the goods or property of an enemy nation or of individuals employed by an enemy nation.

Longboat. Also known as a jolly boat or barge, the longboat was the primary means of moving men and equipment between a large ship and the shore or between two large ships. Longboats ranged from twenty to twenty-eight feet long and averaged between seven and nine feet wide. Although some longboats were fitted with detachable masts and could be rigged for sail, their primary means of propulsion was by oar. Longboat oarsmen rowed in pairs, with two individuals manning each of the boat's six to eight pairs of oars. A longboat crew generally consisted of the required number of oarsmen plus one officer manning the tiller (located in the rear of the boat), which steered the craft. When necessary, a longboat could also accommodate as many passengers as oarsmen, bringing the largest longboat's capacity to thirty-three men.

Man-of-war or man-o'-war. A heavily armed, three-masted warship with square-rigged sails, the man-of-war (also spelled man-o'-war) was the primary battleship from the mid-seventeenth to early nineteenth century. A full-size man-of-war could be up to two hundred feet in length and carry anywhere from seventy-four to a hundred cannons mounted on three tiers of gun decks.

Periagua. In the Caribbean and on the Eastern Seaboard of North America, periagua (from the Spanish word *piragua*, in turn derived from the Carib-language term for dugout), formerly referred to a range of small craft, including canoes and sailing vessels. By the eighteenth century, the term was applied to flat-bottomed boats that had one or two masts and could also be rowed. These boats could be thirty feet or more long and carried up to thirty men.

Pink. In the Atlantic Ocean, pink (derived from the Dutch word *pincke*) referred to any small ship with a narrow stern. Pinks had a large cargo capacity and were generally square rigged. Their flat bottoms and resulting shallow draft made them more useful in shallow waters than some similar classes of ship. They were most often used for short-range missions in protected channels, as both merchant vessels and warships. A number saw service in the Royal Navy during the second half of the seventeenth century. This style of ship was often used in the Mediterranean because it could navigate in shallow waters and through coral reefs. It could also be maneuvered up rivers and streams. Contrary to popular thought, the pink is quite a fast and flexible ship.

Pinnace. The term *pinnace* could refer to two different types of marine craft. The first was a small vessel used as a "tender" to larger vessels, among other things, and the second was a ship-rigged vessel popular in northern waters in the seventeenth through nineteenth centuries. The smaller pinnace was a lightweight boat, propelled by sails or oars, formerly used as a tender for guiding merchant and war vessels. In modern parlance, *pinnace* has come to mean a boat associated with some kind of larger vessel that doesn't fit under the launch or lifeboat definitions. In general, the pinnace had sails and was employed to ferry messages between ships-of-the-line, visit harbors ahead of the fleet with messages of state, pick up mail, and so on. Pinnaces were also widely used during the pirate-infested seventeenth century, mostly in the Caribbean area. The Spanish favored them as lightweight smuggling vessels, whereas the Dutch preferred them as raiders. Pirates frequently employed them as scouts and for night attacks, since they were small, reliable, and extremely quick, even against the wind. The second, larger type was developed by the Dutch during the early seventeenth century. It had a hull form resembling a small "race-built" galleon and was usually rigged as a ship (square rigged on three masts) or carried a similar rig on two masts, in a fashion akin to the later brig. Pinnaces saw use as merchant vessels, pirate vessels, and small warships. Not all were small vessels, some being nearer to larger ships in tonnage. This type saw widespread use in northern waters, mainly by the Dutch.

Rigging. Rigging as a general term describes both the ropes and block and tackle used to control and support the sails of a ship. Sailing ships of the seventeenth and eighteenth centuries carried their sails in one of two manners: either square rigged or fore-and-aft rigged. In the fore-and-aft rig, the sails were arranged to stand along the length of the ship, from bow to stern, whereas in the square-rig arrangement, the sails ran perpendicularly across the ship from port to starboard (left to right). Large warships and merchant ships with three masts were almost universally square rigged, because this type of arrangement tended to work better on the long sea voyages for which they were designed. Small ships, such as sloops and schooners, were normally fore-and-aft rigged for greater maneuverability. On some vessels, such as cutters, a combination of square and fore-and-aft rigging was used. In other cases, the type of rigging determined the ship's designation; for example, when square rigged, some two-masted ships were known as brigantines, but when the same ships carried a combination of square and fore-and-aft rigging, they were called brigs.

Schooner. Schooners were medium-size, two-masted ships that were usually fore-and-aft rigged. Almost as fast and maneuverable as sloops, schooners were a particular favorite in the American coastal mercantile trade, and they adapted well for privateering use. Easily manned by small crews, schooners tended to be between 120 and 160 feet long and from 32 to 36 feet wide. They were shallow drafted, with a depth below the

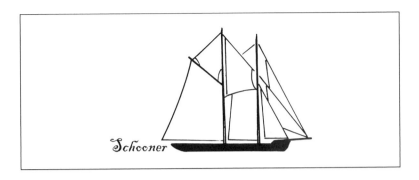

Schooner

waterline of 10 to 14 feet, making them easy to navigate in shallow rivers and inlets, where larger ships could not follow. An armed privateer schooner could carry six to ten small-bore cannons on its main deck.

Ship-of-the-line. The largest of the men-of-war, Britain's ships-of-the-line were the largest, most dangerous vessels afloat. A ship-of-the-line could carry 74 to 124 cannons on three gun decks, although the most common (about fifty percent of the Royal Navy) carried only 74 guns, with 36 located on each side of the ship on the gun decks, and two on the top deck. The size and weight of a ship-of-the-line allowed it to carry a preponderance of heavy cannons, ranging in size from thirty-two- to forty-two-pounders. A typical ship-of-the-line during the mid-eighteenth century had a crew of more than eight hundred men. Ships-of-the-line got their name from the battle tactic wherein the vessels in a fleet would form in a long line, rather than be confined in a cluster, so that they could sail past an enemy one after the other, raking an enemy ship with an unbroken line of fire.

Sloop. A sloop was a small, easily maneuvered, fore-and-aft-rigged ship with a single mast requiring only a small crew to man. The sloop was distinguished from a cutter by the position of its mast, which was located only about one-third of the ship's length behind the bow, placing it farther forward than the cutter's mast. The sloop generally carried three sails: a large main sail, extending to the back of the mast, and two triangular sails running from the mast to the front of the ship. Sloops could

Sloop

range in length from thirty to sixty feet. Although a sloop could carry only six to ten small cannons, its speed and maneuverability allowed it to attack and outrun larger ships with heavier armament.

Swivel gun. Small, portable cannons mounted on Y-shaped forks, swivel guns were usually less than three feet long and normally had bores of one and a quarter inches. A swivel gun could fire either a single ball or a handful of grapeshot. The butt end of the gun was usually fitted with a wooden handle so that the gunner could easily turn and aim the gun after dropping the bottom leg of the fork into a hole in a ship's railing or an oarlock on a whaleboat or longboat. Relatively lightweight, the swivel gun could be carried by one man from one side of a ship to the other or onto a whaleboat or longboat.

Tonnage. A ship's tonnage refers to its size. It does not describe the weight of the ship, but is a measurement of the amount of water the ship displaces based on the fact that a hundred cubic feet of seawater weighs one Imperial British long-ton (tonne), or 2,240 pounds. Because a ship rides lower in the water when fully loaded than it does when empty—and therefore displaces more water—the tonnage is calculated when the craft is fully loaded.

Whaleboat. The fast and highly maneuverable whaleboat's speed was aided by its shallow draft and the fact that it was pointed at both ends like a canoe. An additional advantage of the double prow (points on both ends) was the fact that the whaleboat did not have to be turned around to reverse direction—the oarsmen could simply turn around in their seats and continue rowing. Whaleboats were all propelled by oars rather than sails. Originally designed to be carried on whaling ships and lowered into the water when a whale was sighted, the whaleboat adapted wonderfully to coastal privateering. Enhancing the whaleboat's ability to hide from pursuers was its retractable keel, which allowed it to navigate shallow rivers, shoals, and sandbar-filled coastal waters where larger, deeper vessels could not follow. Averaging thirty-six feet in length, the whaleboats could be manned by as few as six men but, as needs dictated, could carry as many as twenty-four.

Bibliography

Bonner, Willard Haliam. *Pirate Laureate: The Life and Legends of Captain Kidd*. New Brunswick, NJ: Rutgers University Press, 1947.

Burney, James (Capt.). *History of the Buccaneers of America*. London: Payne and Foss, 1816.

Cawthorne, Nigel. *Pirates: An Illustrated History*. Great Malvern, England: Capella Publishing, 2005.

Coggleshall, George. *History of the American Privateers and Letters of Marque During our War with England in the Years 1812, '13, and '14*. New York: Putnam, 1861.

Cordingly, David. *Life Among the Pirates: The Romance and the Reality*. New York: Little Brown and Company, 1995.

———. *Under The Black Flag: The Romance and Reality of Life Among the Pirates*. London: Harcourt Brace & Co., 1995.

Crooker, William S. *Pirates of the North Atlantic*. Halifax, NS, Canada: Nimbus Publishing, 2004.

Dampier, William. *Piracy, Turtles & Flying Foxes*. 1686. Reprint, London: Penguin Books.

Diehl, Daniel, and Mark Donnelly. *How Did They Manage? Leadership Secrets of History*. London: Spiro Press, 2002.

Donnelly, Mark, and Daniel Diehl. *Pirates of New Jersey: Plunder and High Adventure on the Garden State Coastline*. Mechanicsburg, PA: Stackpole Books, 2010.

Earle, Peter. *The Pirate Wars*. New York: Methuen Books, 2004.

Ellms, Charles. *Pirates: Authentic Narratives of the Lives, Exploits, and Executions of the World's Most Infamous Buccaneers*. New York: Random House Value, 1996.

Exquemelin, Alexander. *The Buccaneers of America*. New York: Dover Publications, 1969.

Gilbert, Henry. *Pirates: True Tales of Notorious Buccaneers*. New York: Dover Publications, 2008.

Grosse, Philip. *The Pirates' Who's Who: Giving Particulars Of The Lives and Deaths Of The Pirates And Buccaneers.* New York: Burt Franklin, 1924.

Herrmann, Oscar. *Pirates and Piracy.* New York: Stettiner Brothers, 1902.

Johnson, Captain Charles. *A General History of the Robberies & Murders of the Most Notorious Pirates.* 1724. Reprint, London: Conway Maritime Press, 1998.

Lewis, Jon E., ed. *The Mammoth Book of Pirates.* London: Constable Robinson, 2006.

Little, Benerson. *The Sea Rover's Practice: Pirate Tactics and Techniques, 1630–1730.* Washington, DC: Potomac Books, 2005.

Lucie-Smith, Edward. *Outcasts of the Sea: Pirates and Piracy.* New York: Paddington Press, 1978.

Maclay, Edward Stanton. *A History of American Privateers.* New York: D. Appleton and Company, 1899.

Masefield, John. *On the Spanish Main: Or, some English Forays on the Isthmus of Darien.* London: Methuen and Co., 1906.

Mitchell, David. *Pirates.* London: Book Club Associates, 1976.

Nash, Jay Robert. *The Encyclopedia of World Crime.* New York: Crime Books, 1990.

Norman, C. B. *The Corsairs of France.* London: Searle & Rivington, 1887.

Patton, Robert H. *Patriot Pirates: The Privateer War for Freedom and Fortune in the American Revolution.* New York: Pantheon Books, 2008.

Pirotta, Saviour. *Pirates and Treasures.* Andover, Hampshire, UK: Thomson Learning, 1995.

Platt, Richard. *Pirate.* New York: Alfred A. Knopf, 1994.

Pyle, Howard. *Howard Pyle's Book of Pirates.* New York: Dover Books, 2000.

Pyle, Howard, ed. *The Buccaneers and Marooners of America.* London: T. Fisher Unwin, 1892.

Rediker, Marcus. *Villains of All Nations: Atlantic Pirates in the Golden Age.* Boston: Beacon Press, 2004.

Roberts, Nancy. *Blackbeard and Other Pirates of the Atlantic Coast.* Winston-Salem, NC: John F. Blair Publisher, 1995.

Rogers, Captain Woodes. *Life Aboard a British Privateer in the time of Queen Anne.* London: Chapman and Hall, 1889.

Rogozinski, Jan. *Honor Among Thieves: Captain Kidd, Henry Every, and the Pirate Democracy in the Indian Ocean.* Mechanicsburg, PA: Stackpole Books, 2000.

Seitz, Don C. *Under the Black Flag: Exploits of the Most Notorious Pirates.* New York: The Dial Press, 1925.

Shomette, Donald G. *Pirates on the Chesapeake: Being a True History of Pirates, Picaroons, and Raiders on Chesapeake Bay, 1610–1807.* Centreville, MD: Tidewater Publishers, 1985.

Stark, Francis R. *The Abolition of Privateering and the Declaration of Paris.* New York: Columbia University, 1897.

Stivers, Reuben Elmore. *Privateers and Volunteers*. Annapolis, MD: Naval Institute Press, 1975.

Stockton, Frank R. *Buccaneers and Pirates of our Coasts.* London: Macmillian and Co., 1919.

Thornbury, Walter. *The Monarchs of the Main*. London: Routledge, 1861.

Winston, Alexander. *Pirates and Privateers*. London: Arrow Books, 1969.

Woodard, Colin. *The Republic of Pirates*. New York: Harcourt Brace, 2007.

Zacks, Richard. *The Pirate Hunter: The True Story of Captain Kidd*. New York: Hyperion Books, 2002.

ONLINE SOURCES

Benford, Timothy B. "Rep. Alan Benny's Clues to Pirate Captain Kidd's Treature." *Yahoo! Voices*, October 30, 2007. http://voices.yahoo.com/rep-alan-bennys-clues-pirate-captain-kidds-treasure-619062.html.

"Famous Pirates and Buccaneers." *Blacksheep Ancestors*. http://www.blacksheepancestors.com/pirates/.

Guthrie, Robert. "The Trial of Captain Kidd: The Fate of the Notorious Pirate, William Kidd." *American History @ Suite 101*. http://colonial-america.suite101.com/article.cfm/the_trial_of_captain_kidd.

"Pirates & Privateers: Captain Kidd." *The Best of Legends*. http://bestoflegends.org/pirates/kidd.html.

Stockton, Frank Richard. "The Real Captain Kidd." *The Pirate's Realm*. http://www.thepiratesrealm.com/Captain%20Kidd%20Stockton.html.

Other Titles in the
Pirates Series

by Mark P. Donnelly & Daniel Diehl

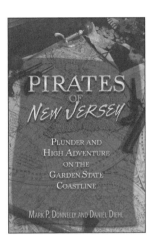 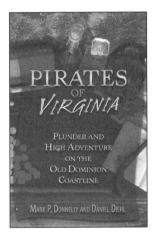

Pirates of New Jersey
978-0-8117-0667-4

Pirates of Virginia
978-0-8117-1036-7

WWW.STACKPOLEBOOKS.COM
1-800-732-3669